AF262762

GOYA'S
FORGE

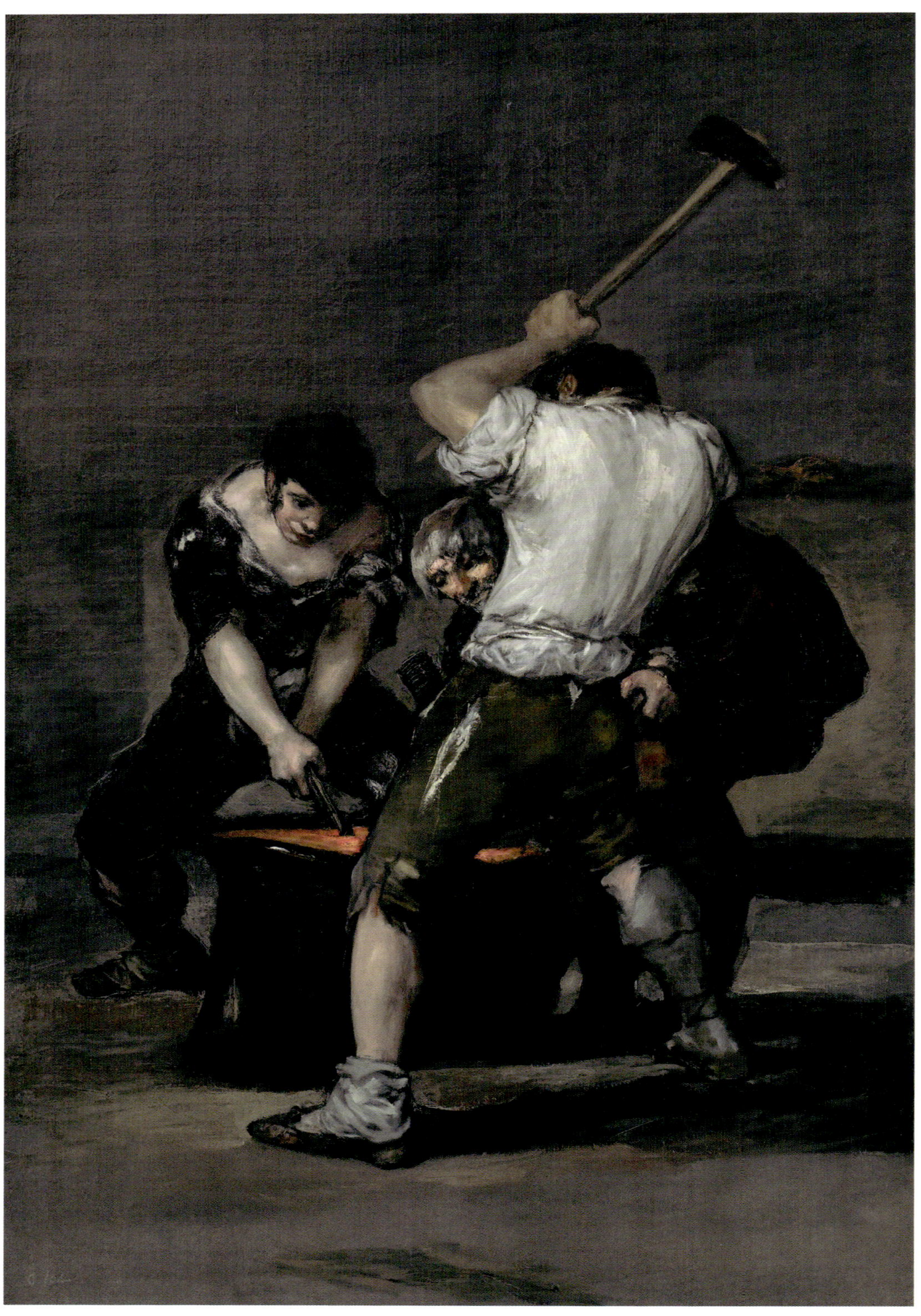

GOYA'S *FORGE*

Hisham Matar
Xavier F. Salomon

The Frick Collection, New York
in association with D Giles Limited

FRICK DIPTYCH SERIES

Designed to foster critical engagement and interest specialist and non-specialist alike, each book in this series illuminates a single work in the Frick's rich collection with an essay by a Frick curator paired with a contribution from a contemporary artist or writer.

First published in 2025 by The Frick Collection
1 East 70th Street
New York, NY 10021
www.frick.org

Michaelyn Mitchell, Editor in Chief
Gemma McElroy, Assistant Editor

In association with GILES
An imprint of D Giles Limited
66 High Street
Lewes, BN7 1XG, UK
gilesltd.com

Copyedited and proofread by Sarah Kane
Designed by Caroline and Roger Hillier,
The Old Chapel Graphic Design

Produced by GILES

Printed and bound in China

A CIP catalogue record for this book is available from the Library of Congress.

ISBN 978-1-913875-52-7

Cover and pages 6 and 18: details from Francisco de Goya y Lucientes, *The Forge*, ca. 1815–20 (frontispiece)

Frontispiece: Francisco de Goya y Lucientes, *The Forge*, ca. 1815–20. Oil on canvas, 71½ × 49¼ in. (181.6 × 125.1 cm). The Frick Collection, New York; Henry Clay Frick Bequest

Distributed in the USA and Canada by
Consortium Book Sales & Distribution
The Keg House
34 Thirteenth Avenue, NE, Suite 101
Minneapolis, MN 55413-1007
USA
www.cbsd.com

CONTENTS

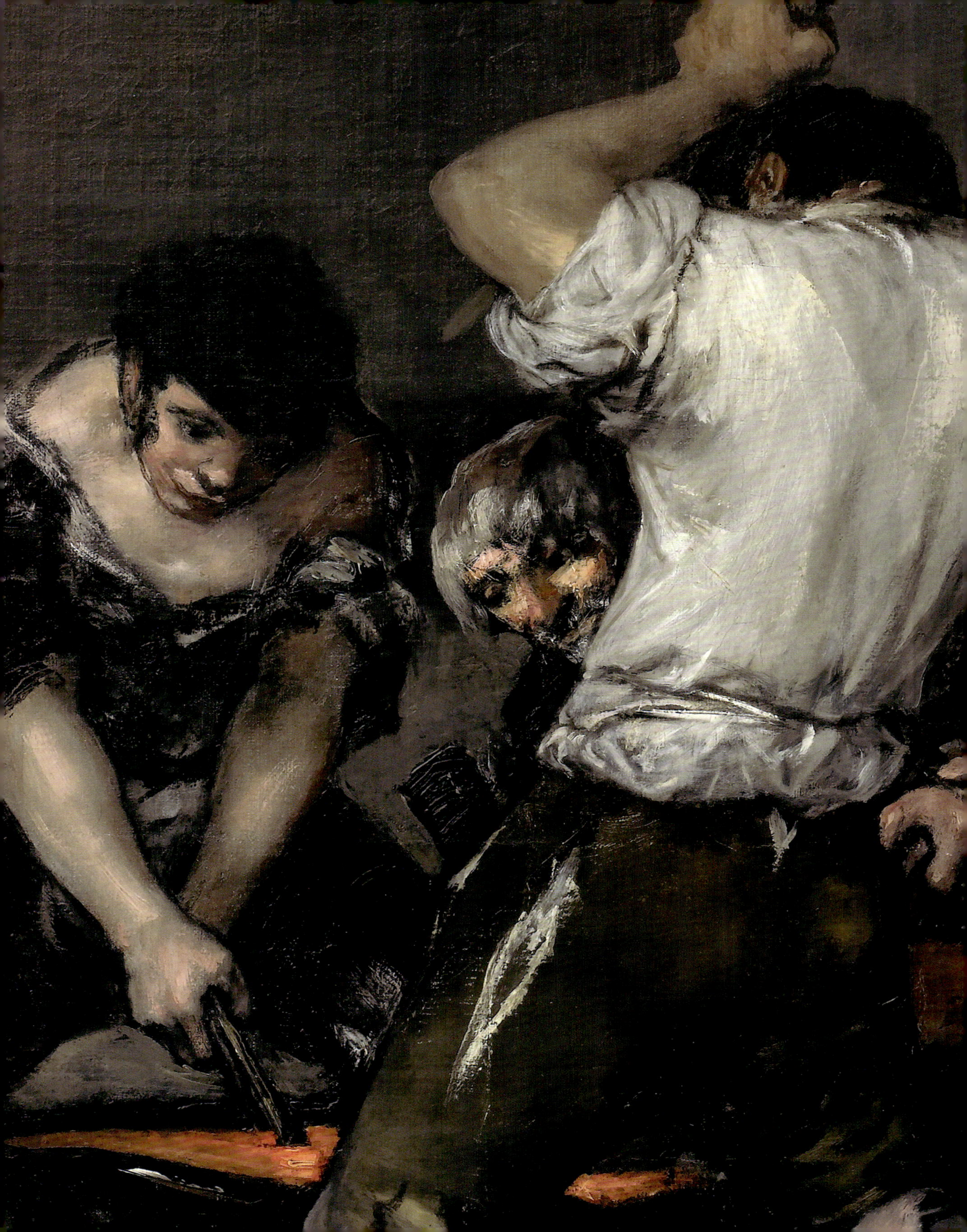

A monumental scene of three men manipulating red-hot metal, Goya's *Forge* evokes narratives of the forge of Vulcan, where Vulcan and his assistants created armor and weapons for his fellow gods. The painting's intended meaning, however, remains unknown. Also unknown is the reason that Henry Clay purchased it, given that his daughter, Helen Clay Frick, wrote that her father only collected works "that were pleasant to live with." One might very well want to live with this compelling masterpiece by "an artist of enigmatic mind and permanent significance"—as Peter Schjeldahl described him—but probably not because it is "pleasant."

In this fifteenth volume of the Frick's Diptych series, Xavier F. Salomon, Deputy Director and Peter Jay Sharp Chief Curator, delves into *The Forge*'s fascinating history, its iconographic sources, and its place in Goya's life and work. Salomon's exploration of the Pittsburgh steel industry and Frick's important—if controversial—role in its history frames the painting as a commemorative image of the labor on which Frick's fortune was built. In a lyrical essay, Hisham Matar considers the three figures as the three ages of man, captured, as Henri Cartier-Bresson intoned, at "the decisive moment" in their collaborative work. To both contributors, we owe our deepest thanks.

Thanks are also due to Editor in Chief Michaelyn Mitchell, who managed the production of the publication and, with Assistant Editor Gemma McElroy, edited the text. We would also like to express our gratitude to our publishing partner, D Giles Limited.

Ian Wardropper
Anna-Maria and Stephen Kellen Director, The Frick Collection

ACKNOWLEDGMENTS

I would like to acknowledge quite a few people for their support, assistance, and counsel in my writing of this Diptych. First, I am honored to have Hisham Matar, a writer I profoundly admire, as my co-author. His essay is a beautiful and thoughtful reading of Goya's art, and *The Forge* in particular.

At the Frick, I would like to thank, first and foremost, Ian Wardropper, Anna-Maria and Stephen Kellen Director, as well as Betty Eveillard and the board of trustees. Michaelyn Mitchell, along with Gemma McElroy, has flawlessly, as always, edited this text and improved it in innumerable ways. Alice Spadini has assisted me on this project, and I would like to acknowledge her many contributions. My thanks go to André Onofre Limírio Chaves—an Ayesha Bulchandani Intern at the Frick in the summer of 2023—who helped to gather material on Goya's *Forge*. I would also like to acknowledge my colleagues Aimee Ng, Marie-Laure Buku Pongo, and Giulio Dalvit for always being inspiring and encouraging. Thanks also to the archives team at the Frick, in particular Sally Brazil, Susan Chore, and Julie Ludwig. A special thank you to Rachel Himes and Caitlin F. Henningsen, for discussions regarding their wonderful essay published in the *Journal of Museum Education* in 2020. Over the years, I have had the pleasure of looking at many of Goya's paintings and discussing them with the Frick's Curator Emerita, Susan Grace Galassi, who has contributed so much to Goya studies.

Esteemed Goya scholars and friends—Véronique Gerard Powell, Mark McDonald, and Janis A. Tomlinson—were kind enough to read drafts of my essay and provide comments and corrections. Over the years, it has been an honor to discuss Goya with them and to learn from their extraordinary work. Any mistakes, of course, are entirely mine. For the past decade or so, I have been fortunate to have been able to discuss Goya's technique with Dorothy Mahon in the Paintings Conservation Department at the Metropolitan Museum of Art. Dorothy also read a draft of the essay and, as always, provided invaluable information and advice. Bruno Mottin was kind in sharing with me his technical studies on many Goya paintings in French public collections, in particular *The Young Women* from the Palais des Beaux-Arts in Lille. For all his knowledge on the steel industry in Pittsburgh, for several eye-opening tours of Carrie Blast Furnaces, and for having read parts of my essay, I would like to thank Ron Baraff, Director of Historic Resources & Facilities at Rivers of

Steel in Pittsburgh. My thanks also go to Sofia Barroso, Donatienne Dujardin, Cordélia Hattori, Peter Pininski, and Guy Stair Sainty.

Most of this essay was envisioned and written in Warsaw over Christmas 2023. I would like to thank M for all his support, always irreplaceable and essential. Every step of this project was discussed and explored with him.

Xavier F. Salomon
Deputy Director and Peter Jay Sharp Chief Curator, The Frick Collection

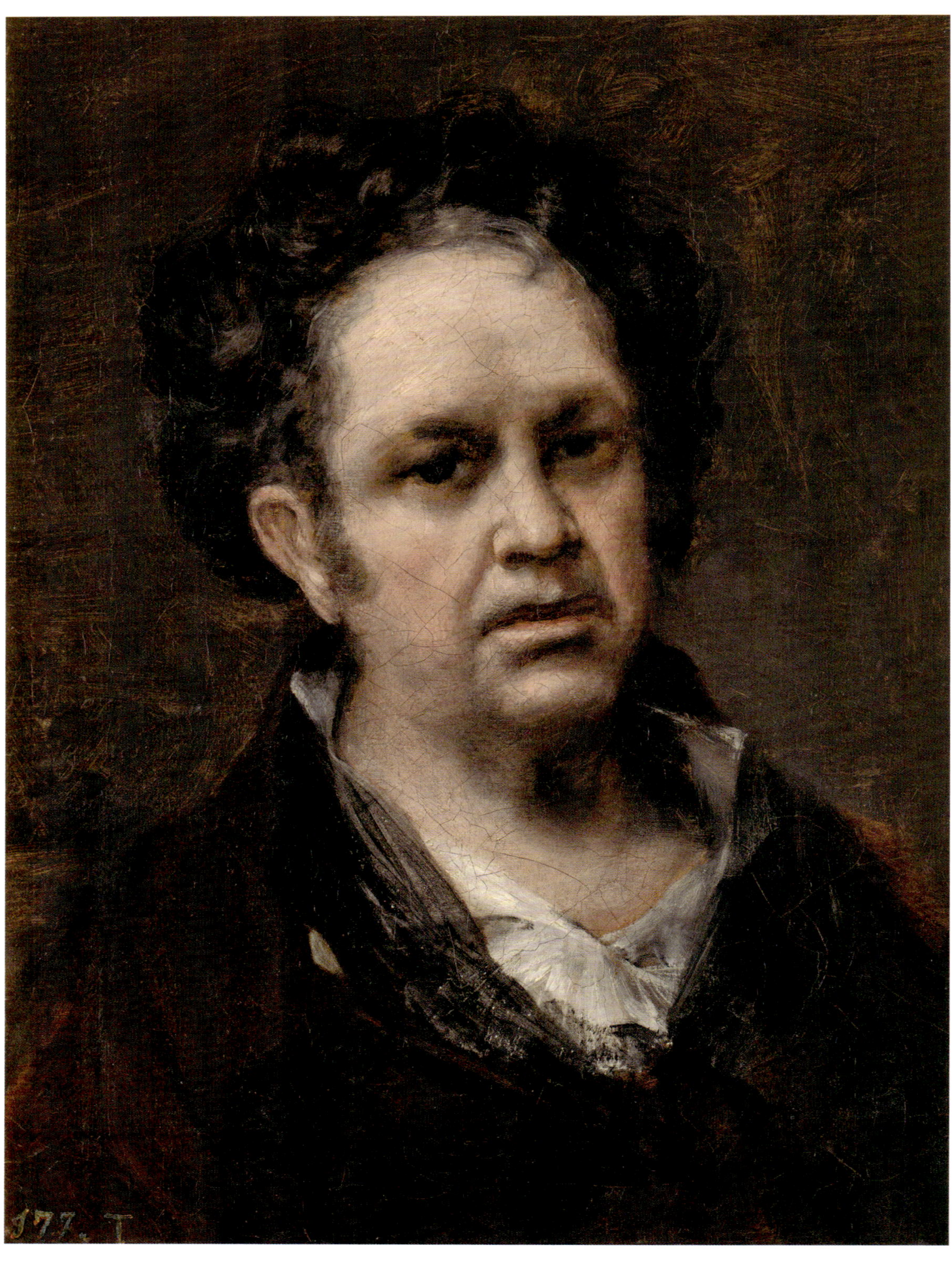

ON FRANCISCO GOYA'S *FORGE*

Hisham Matar

Francisco Goya had a good face, round and telling, a taking and giving face, one to draw as well as to be drawn to. In a self-portrait from 1815, when the painter was sixty-nine, he appears to be contending with the fact that he is at once exposed and veiled. This is a face, he seems to be thinking to himself, that would give me up in an instant, a face I can hope to have as much command over as I do the surface of the sea. Here is me and there is my face, and given the distance between the two, he seems to be asking, how is one to proceed? What are the possibilities of self-knowledge when everything that we are happens outside of our command, is formed and moved, very much like a sea, by its own system of inner currents? His hair is pushed back, playing its part in this conspiracy of revelation. His eyes are tired but engaged, thinking, wanting and perhaps a little jealous and inquisitive too, as though what he is seeing are also his younger faces and those yet to come. His mouth is cautious, fearful that any sort of utterance might break the spell. It is a portrait of a man who is as ambivalent about the usefulness of words as he is about his own authority over any given subject, including himself.

Such ungovernable states fascinated Goya. By this stage in his career, that concern turns ever so intimately to the subject of aging. Two decades before this picture, and due to a mysterious illness that no one could diagnose, and, therefore, must have seemed pointedly decreed by Divine will, he had gone deaf. Yet in the portrait, one can sense him straining to hear. As well as everything else that is going on in that picture, it suddenly appears as a study of loss and survival. Three years earlier, his wife of forty years, Josefa Bayeu—his nickname for her was Pepa—passed away. The couple had seven children.

Francisco de Goya y Lucientes
Self-Portrait, 1815
Oil on canvas
18 × 14 in. (45.8 × 35.6 cm)
Museo Nacional del Prado, Madrid

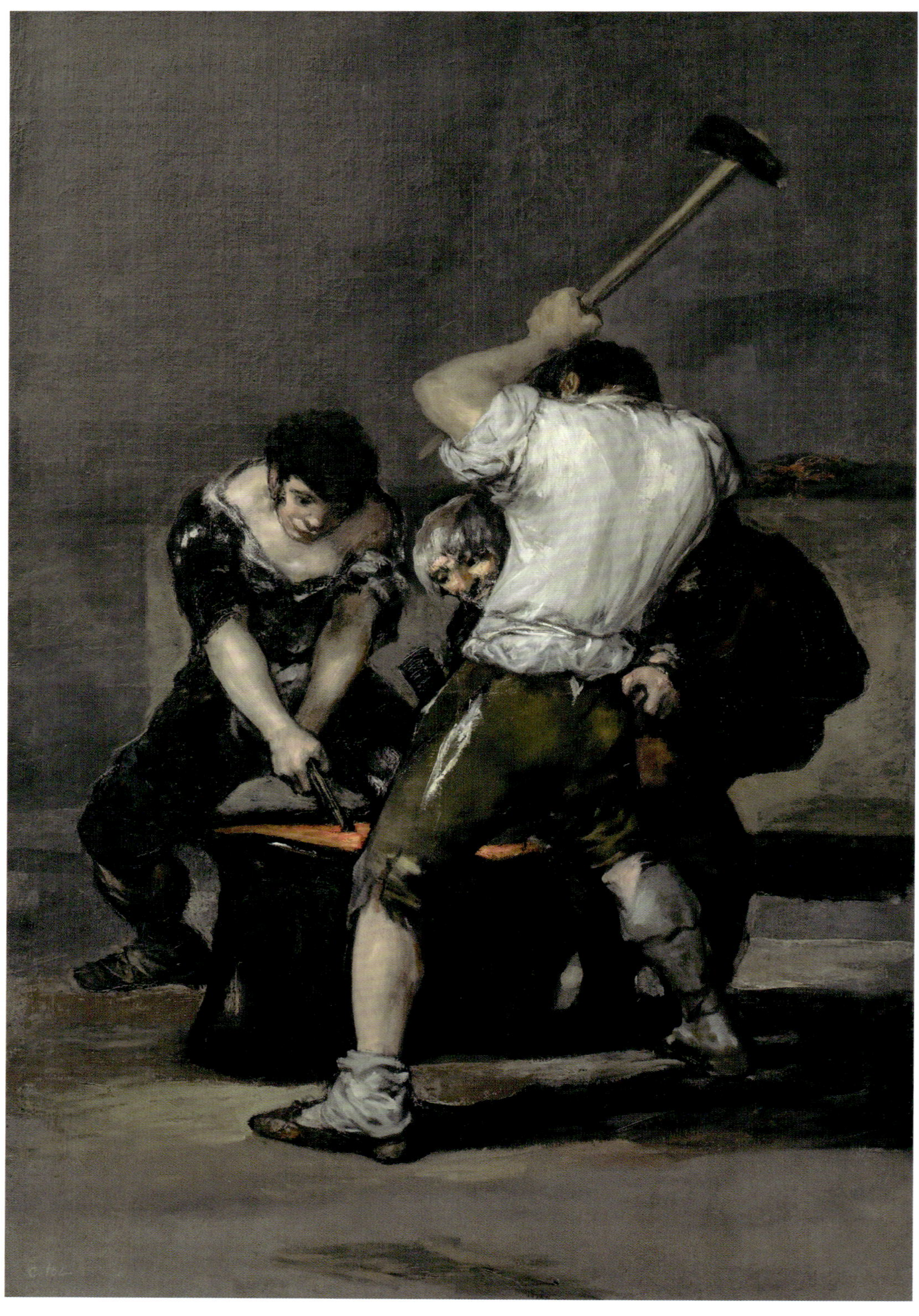

All but one died in infancy. The fact that he was still there, capable of looking straight at himself, must have seemed a dark and unlikely victory.

Around the same time that he painted the self-portrait, perhaps even concurrently, he worked on another picture named *The Forge*. Its subject, three collaborating smiths, each ferociously locked into the demands of his task, is in direct contrast to its large size, one more usually reserved for stately portraits and scenes of a religious or mythological nature. When you stand in front of it, its scale, but also the way space and perspective are managed, makes the men appear nearly life size. Goya freezes them mid-action, in what the photographer Henri Cartier-Bresson famously termed "the decisive moment." In fact, the pictorial logic is much closer to that of a twentieth-century photograph than it is to an early nineteenth-century Romantic painting. And as in a photograph, part of what draws us in, part of the enjoyment we derive, is the ability to study, for as long as we wish, a fleeting instant captured in a still frame, a moment that we know passed in a glimpse, one never intended for posterity and, therefore, like in a Cartier-Bresson or, perhaps closer to Goya, Brassaï photograph, there is the sense that what we are being offered has been salvaged from oblivion. What is deeply modern about Goya is that, like Brassaï and many other later artists, he believed that the more modest the subject and more passing the instant, the more profound the effect. Instead of seeking to impress us with the status of his protagonists, Goya focuses on the impressive stature of human life caught in work and time.

The picture references *Vulcan's Forge*, from 1630, by Diego Velázquez. Goya's compatriot had been an abiding inspiration, a figure to at times emulate and at others revolt against. But perhaps the painting that was uppermost on his mind here was *Venus at Vulcan's Forge*, an earlier picture from 1560–64, by the prominent Flemish artist Frans Floris the Elder. Goya organizes his three figures in much the same way. The radical turn is that he empties their surroundings, erasing any reference to God or nature or society, rendering the men's activity severely solitary and all the more allegorical for it.

Goya's smiths gather around a blistering flame, almost lava-like, shunning all distraction. Their surroundings appear less as an interior or a landscape and more as a graying and absenting state of mind. Their focus resembles Goya's and, in turn, ours. We are all conspiring around the fire. If our eye wanders beyond the main scene, it is quickly smothered into the bleak and unsteady background. There is hardly any distinction between ground,

Francisco de Goya y Lucientes
The Forge, ca. 1815–20
(frontispiece)

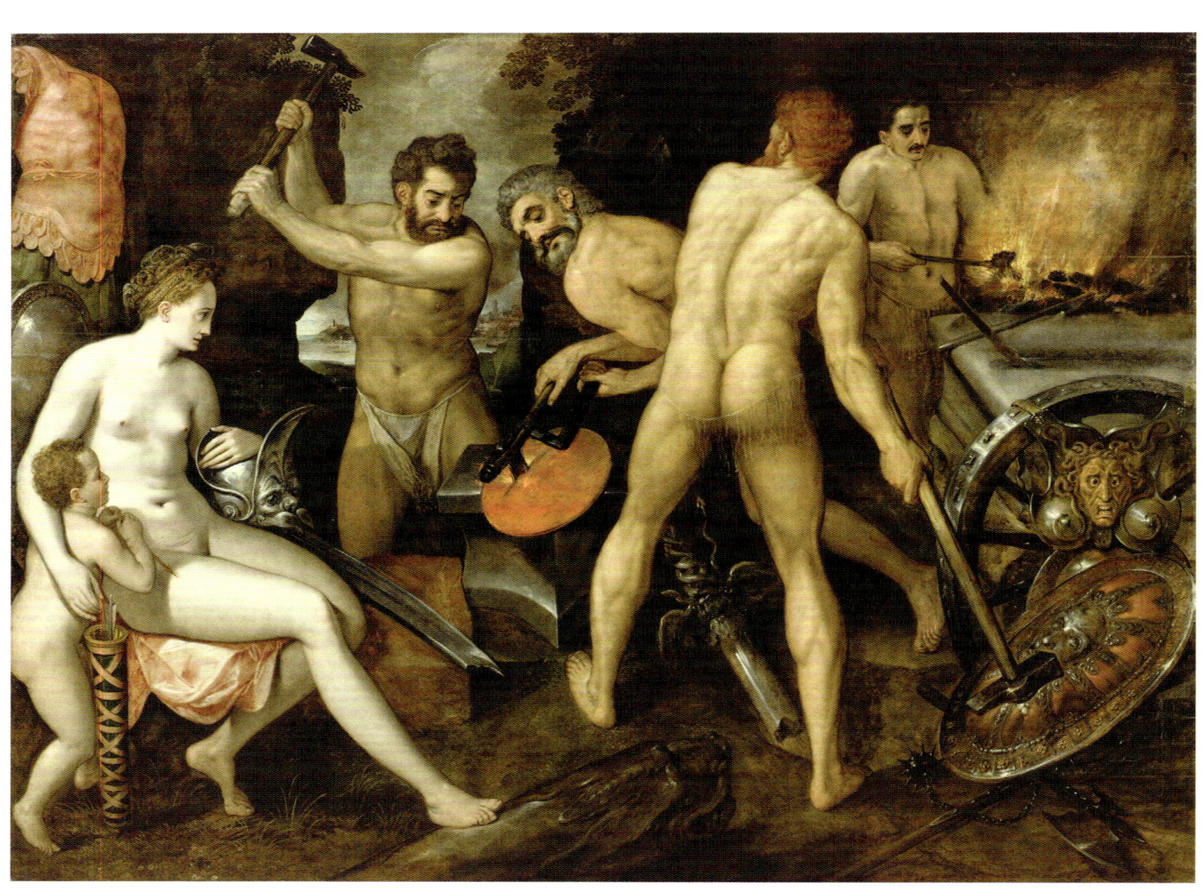

mid-distance, and sky, and the muted hues move and appear to be both haunted and haunting. All nature has dissolved. The world and all that it contains have been, for this moment, forfeited for a single purpose. It is a background that is the color of neglect and indifference.

It is not complicated to build a forge. With basic materials, magic is made. A brick or stone structure where a fire at the center can be fanned vertically. A hammer and an anvil to strike the red-hot iron. In contrast to these basic tools, a complex human ingenuity is required: artistry and a refined skill, as well as strength and stamina. The work is both brutal and fine and can induce, in its practitioners, a particular mesmeric quality. If you have ever manned a forge, you would know what I mean. The concentrated heat is the ferocious heart. It burns your face and chest and thighs. At times you feel your shoulders swell from the temperature. It is both unbearable and alluring. You are shaping metal and cannot help but suspect that a vague and elusive part of you is also being molded.

Perhaps because of this, most depictions of forges in art—and there have been a few—are aware of the magnetic force of the subject, as though suspecting that men and women can become just as vulnerable to the allure as moths. The flame is the kernel, and you are, for those seconds before the metal reaches the right temperature, a suspended observer. Goya is interested in this, in the three men's collaboration with the fire, and, even from within the bustle, they look as though caught in a fervent and lonesome prayer.

This is perhaps connected to the artist's decision to have each of his protagonists resemble one of the three ages of man. First, if we are to read the painting from left to right, there is the innocent youngster with the keen expression. A man not quite yet a man. His will appears tender. He has a face that is yet to truly know itself. And what is honest about it is that it suspects as much. He faces us, looking down at his task, but does so dreamily, almost dangerously. It is the look of a man who has for an instant lost concentration. Is he having second thoughts? The slip could cost him his life. His arms, neck, and the shoulders revealed by his loose shirt are strong and capable, but are new to this work. His complexion has yet to acquire that hard leathery redness of an experienced smith. But he is very keen to learn. I had an uncle who had beautifully large and well-worn hands. As a child, I wanted so much to have hands like his. I imagine this boy too is looking forward to such an accomplishment. And even from within his momentary absentmindedness,

Frans Floris
Venus at Vulcan's Forge, 1560–64
Oil on panel
59 × 78 in. (150 × 198 cm)
Staatliche Museen,
Gemäldegalerie, Berlin

his lips appear to smile hopefully toward the prospect of such a future, one not only filled with good and plentiful labor, but where he would be granted the chance, the gift of time to achieve mastery over his vocation, and, therefore, one day hope to contribute to its tradition and have his own apprentices to train. And perhaps what he is glimpsing now, what has taken his mind wandering, is that golden possibility, resembled, in all of its detail and implications, in the glowing fire and the forming metal. His is a gentle and hopeful faith in that promise. And what more can one want than the honor of honest work.

Beneath him, appearing at an odd angle, one borrowed from Frans Floris's *Forge*, is the face of the old man. His aspect speaks of joys savored and private torments endured. A face that has had time to attempt to manage its affairs, and that, although it has had some measure of success, knows it has failed just as often. This has humbled it, but it has also made it prudent and incredulous. And it is this shrewd distrust, I cannot help believe, that is behind his busy work with the bellows, stoking the fire. His posture, crooked and awkward, belongs to one who knows he is intruding. And that is perhaps how it feels when we are old but remain keen on being useful to the young. His hair, thrown forward either by effort or vanity, in order to conceal the receding line, is mousy gray and lacquered with sweat. The tip of his nose is a reddish pink. His position is precarious. He is too close to the line of the falling hammer. But his hand, wielding the bellows, is well practiced and capable. A hand of a man who has worked a lifetime and continues to be able and willing to provide for his family.

Between the old man's grip and his tilted and almost falling head is the dominant and faceless figure of the main character of the picture. He is both the hero and the villain, and will remain suspended between the two probabilities until his hammer falls. His sleeves are impatiently rolled up high, well above the elbows. Get out of my way, he seems to say. His breeches are battered and torn. His left stocking has already fallen to the ankle, revealing his calf, and the other is beginning to slip down his right leg. He is all deed and effort. His muscular back, floppily covered in a white shirt, is turned to us. The sledgehammer, long and intent, is high in the air, held just at the point where it can recede no further and must now come down. It hangs over the scene like a declaration of fate. It will do its work, but given the arrangement of the figures, to say nothing of the precariousness of human life, it is not clear what that work will be exactly. Anything can happen.

The painting is constructed like a turning wheel. It starts with the unknowing and daydreaming young man, goes to the aged but willful old man, and stops at the middle-aged one, who is, we assume, as strong and knowing as a human being ever hopes to get before the scales shift and experience supersedes strength. And even though we cannot see his face, or perhaps exactly because we cannot see it, we give him ours. We cannot help but stand in his place, and therefore, his dilemma—to act is to live with doubt as to the results of our action—is ours too. Each man is alone and all are caught in the rhythm and consequence of their alliance. And suddenly the portrait-shape of the canvas is no longer an accident.

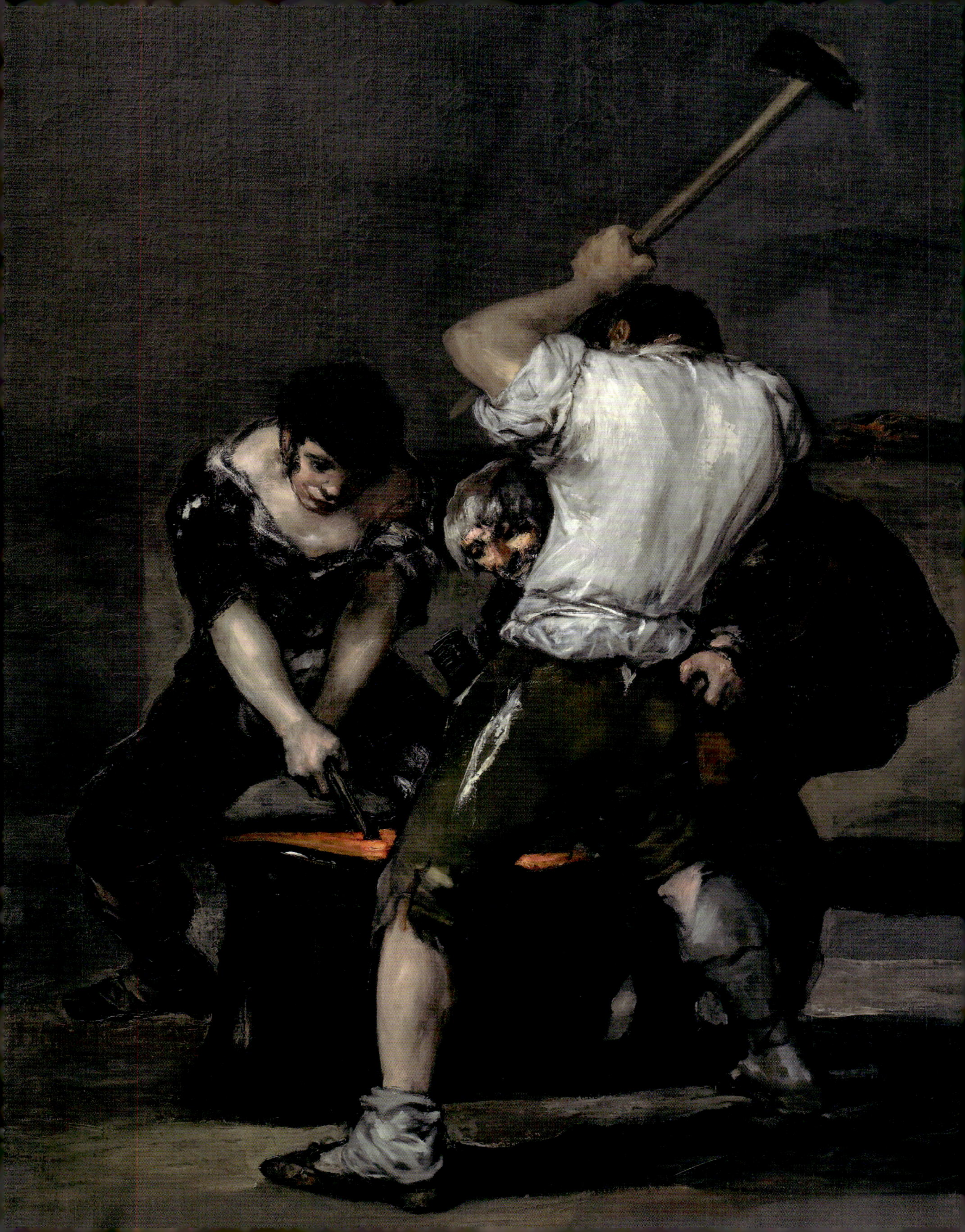

GOYA'S *FORGE*

Xavier F. Salomon

Vedi! Le fosche notturne spoglie / dei cieli sveste l'immensa volta; / sembra una vedova che alfin si toglie / i bruni panni ond'era involta. / All'opra! All'opra / Dàgli, martella. (See! The sky's great vault removes its gloomy, nightly rags; it seems like a widow who at last takes off the dark clothes that enveloped her. To work! To work! Lift up your hammers.)

—Giuseppe Verdi, *Il Trovatore* (Act 2, Scene 1), 1853

The so-called "Anvil Chorus" is one of the most enduringly popular tunes from Giuseppe Verdi's (1813–1901) *Il Trovatore* (*The Troubadour*), first performed at the Teatro Apollo in Rome on January 19, 1853 (fig. 1). Known in Italian as the "Coro degli Zingari" (Gypsy Chorus), the scene, which opens the opera's second act, is a Roma encampment with a chorus of Spanish men forging metal at dawn and hammering on their anvils. The clang of the hammering, as imitated by musical instruments, is one of the most memorable parts of this extraordinary piece of music. Forging is also key to Richard Wagner's (1813–1883) *Ring* (*Der Ring des Nibelungen*), his four-part opera cycle of 1869–76, with significant scenes of smithing in two parts: *Das Rheingold* and *Siegfried*. In a fundamental essay about the image of blacksmiths in nineteenth-century art, Jane Kristof wrote: "the gypsy singers of 'The Anvil Chorus' recall the fact that in southern and eastern Europe the craft was largely dominated by exotic aliens. Still more mysterious are Wagner's Nibelungen, gnomes living in subterranean caverns where they mine and process ores."[1] Throughout the nineteenth century, blacksmiths and forging scenes captured

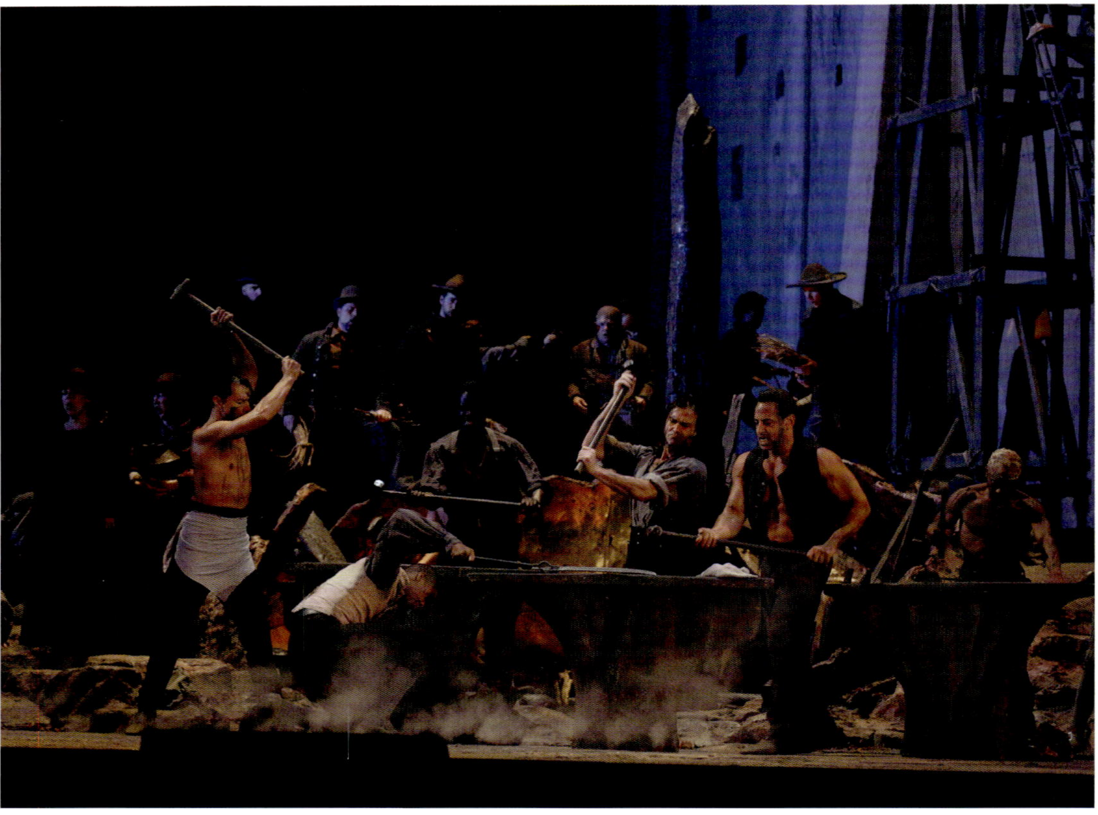

Fig. 1
"Anvil Chorus" from Giuseppe Verdi's *Il Trovatore*, The Metropolitan Opera, New York, 2015

the imagination not only of musicians but also of a number of painters across Europe who depicted scenes both inside and outside forges.

The Forge, by Francisco de Goya y Lucientes (1746–1828), is one of the most iconic images of this topic painted in the first half of the nineteenth century. The subject of this large vertical canvas is set in an ill-defined, gloomy gray space, where a diagonal line in the background seems to imply the presence of a large fireplace, as one would expect in a forge. The floor is also painted in gray and white tones, suggesting beaten earth. Three male figures are grouped around an anvil on which a sheet of metal, reddened by heat, has been placed. In the first catalogue of the Frick's paintings, published in 1916, the figures are described as "a stalwart young man with black curly hair holds the red hot iron with the tongs, a gray-haired man with stubbly beard appears to be holding a cutting-off tool, while the third man, with his back turned to the spectator, is vigorously wielding his sledge."[2] Each man is captured while performing an activity linked to smithing. The man on the left is holding the piece of smelted metal with a pair of tongs, while the man on the right—his legs wide in their stance, echoing the posture of the man in front of him—lifts a large sledgehammer, ready to beat the metal. The older man, between the two, seems to be either holding the metal down or, more likely, operating a pair of bellows, which are hidden by the back of the figure in the foreground. The two men behind the anvil are in dark clothes, mostly in black tones, while the blacksmith in the foreground wears olive-green trousers and a white shirt, the sleeves of which are rolled up to his elbows. In the heat of the forge, the man's socks are sliding down his calves, the sock on his left leg already all the way down to the shoe.

The Forge has been described as "perhaps Goya's masterpiece in America." It is also one of Goya's most enigmatic works.[3] What the painting was meant to signify, for whom it was painted, and why cannot at present be established. Called one of Goya's "remarkable, heroic representations of workers at work,"[4] the painting has been viewed, most commonly, as "a realism with many overtones—loyalty to work and to companions, communion with a common cause, which give it a resonance that lifts it well beyond descriptive realism."[5] Most agree that, in the painting, "Goya celebrates not a specific occasion but a more general theme: human strength and trained skill and perhaps man's ability to work with his fellows with concerted purpose to a common end."[6] For the art critic Robert Hughes (1938–2012), *The Forge* is simply and effectively "a towering symbol of proletarian strength."[7]

The Forge should be examined in the broader context of Goya's life and other work, but the unusual canvas—painted thirty to fifty years before Verdi's and Wagner's operas—should also be seen, as other scholars have noted, as part of a lineage of depictions of blacksmiths and forges. "A naturalist before his time, Goya heralds with this canvas both the *Stone-breakers* of Courbet and the workers of Zola, with the same rejection of good-breeding and bourgeois conventions"; ultimately, *The Forge* is "a canvas that bridges the chasm between Velázquez and Daumier."[8]

Francisco Goya: Life and Works

Francisco José was the fourth of six children of José Benito Goya and Gracia Lucientes.[9] The couple had married in 1736, and Francisco was born on March 30, 1746, in the small hamlet of Fuendetodos in Aragón, about twenty miles southeast of Zaragoza, his mother's hometown. They lived in Zaragoza, where José worked as a gilder, and were probably visiting Fuendetodos—with their children, Rita, Tomás, and Jacinta—when Gracia gave birth to Francisco. A few months after he was born, they were back in Zaragoza.

Apart from two years spent in Italy, between 1769 and 1771, young Goya studied as a painter in Zaragoza, with José Luzán y Martínez (1710–1785). In the early 1770s, Francisco was already active as an artist in Zaragoza, working on murals in the basilica of Nuestra Señora del Pilar and in the Charterhouse of Aula Dei, just outside the city. Many of his early projects were related to the work of two other painters in Zaragoza, Francisco Bayeu y Subías (1734–1795) and his younger brother, Ramón (1744–1793), with whom he collaborated. On July 25, 1773, Goya married the Bayeus' sister, Josefa (1747–1812). Francisco and Josefa were to have seven children, only one of whom—Javier (1784–1854)—survived to adulthood.

By early 1775, Francisco and Josefa were living in Madrid, the Spanish capital, where the Bayeu brothers were working for the Crown. They were all involved with the recently created royal tapestry manufactory—the Real Fábrica de Tapices de Santa Bárbara—and Goya began his long-standing involvement with royal commissions by painting cartoons for the production of tapestries for a number of royal residences. Through his work for the Crown, he came to know and admire the royal collection of paintings, which included masterpieces of Italian and northern Renaissance art, as well as great seventeenth-century examples by Peter Paul Rubens (1577–1640), Luca Giordano (1634–1705), and, most important, Diego Rodríguez de Silva y Velázquez (1599–1660). Between July and December 1778, Goya produced eleven prints after works by Velázquez—mainly portraits and his *Feast of Bacchus* (fig. 2). Goya enjoyed early success. In 1780, he was admitted to the Real Academia de Bellas Artes, and in the 1780s, while continuing to paint cartoons for tapestries, he worked on a number of important commissions, including an altarpiece for the church of San Francisco el Grande in Madrid (1781–83) and many portraits of aristocrats and members of the royal family. On April 25, 1789, Goya received the title of official royal painter—*pintor de cámara*—and his role as a member of the royal household became more prominent into the 1790s. He was, for example, one of those helping with an inventory of the paintings in the royal collection, which was completed on February 25, 1794.

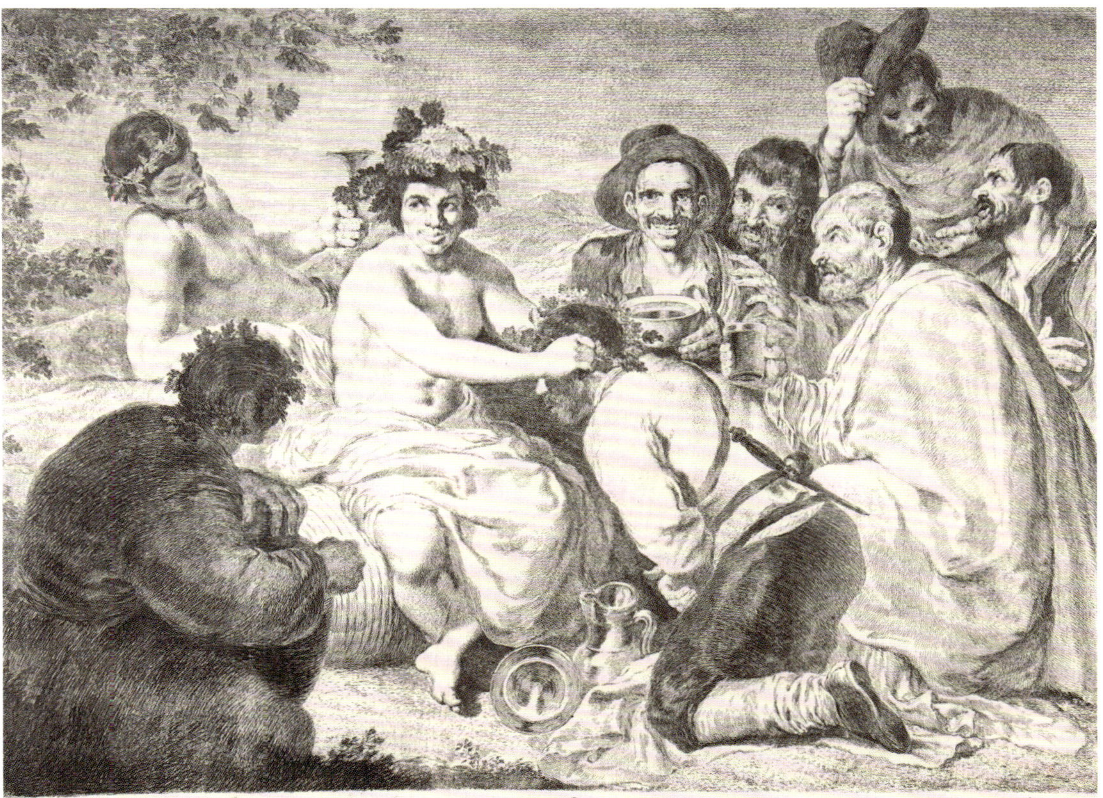

In March 1793, Goya suffered the first of a number of misfortunes. He fell ill while in Seville and was brought by a friend to Cádiz; the mysterious disease left him permanently deaf. For the remaining thirty-five years of his life, Goya lived in absolute silence. It is remarkable that a painting as thunderous as *The Forge* was created by a painter who could only vaguely remember the noise produced in a blacksmith's workshop. Despite his hearing loss, Goya continued to work for the royal family and the Spanish aristocracy. In the 1790s, he became close to the remarkable María del Pilar Teresa Cayetana de Silva y Silva-Bazán, 13th Duchess of Alba (1762–1802), and he painted at least two sensational full-length portraits of her (fig. 3). Around the same time, he worked on both private and prominent public commissions. In 1798, he frescoed the interior of the small church of San Antonio de la Florida; and a year later, he delivered an altarpiece of the *Arrest of Christ* for the Cathedral

Fig. 2
Francisco de Goya y Lucientes, after Diego Rodríguez de Silva y Velázquez
The Feast of Bacchus (*Los borrachos*), 1778
Etching on paper
12⅝ × 17⅛ in.
(320 × 435 mm)
The Metropolitan Museum of Art, New York

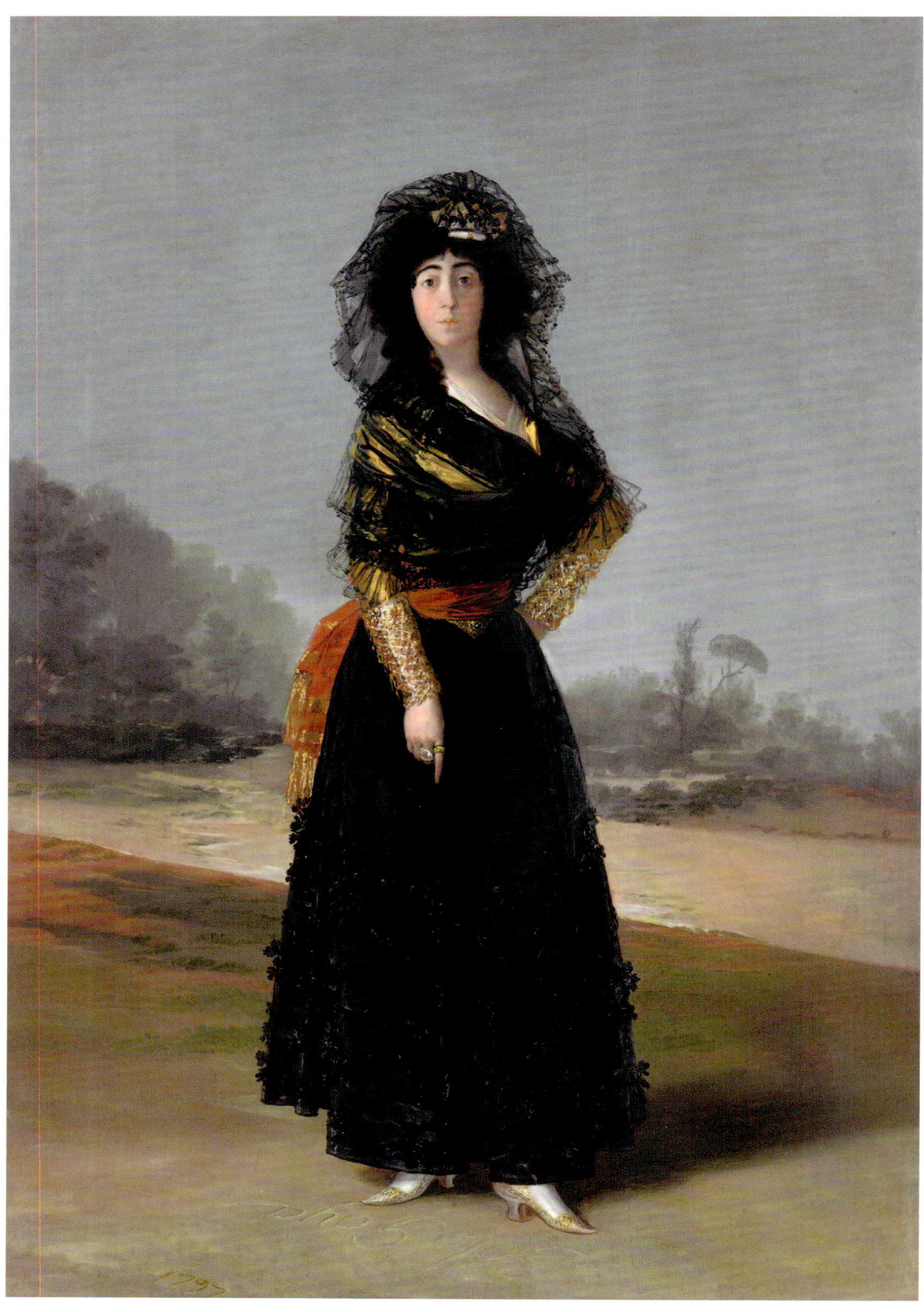

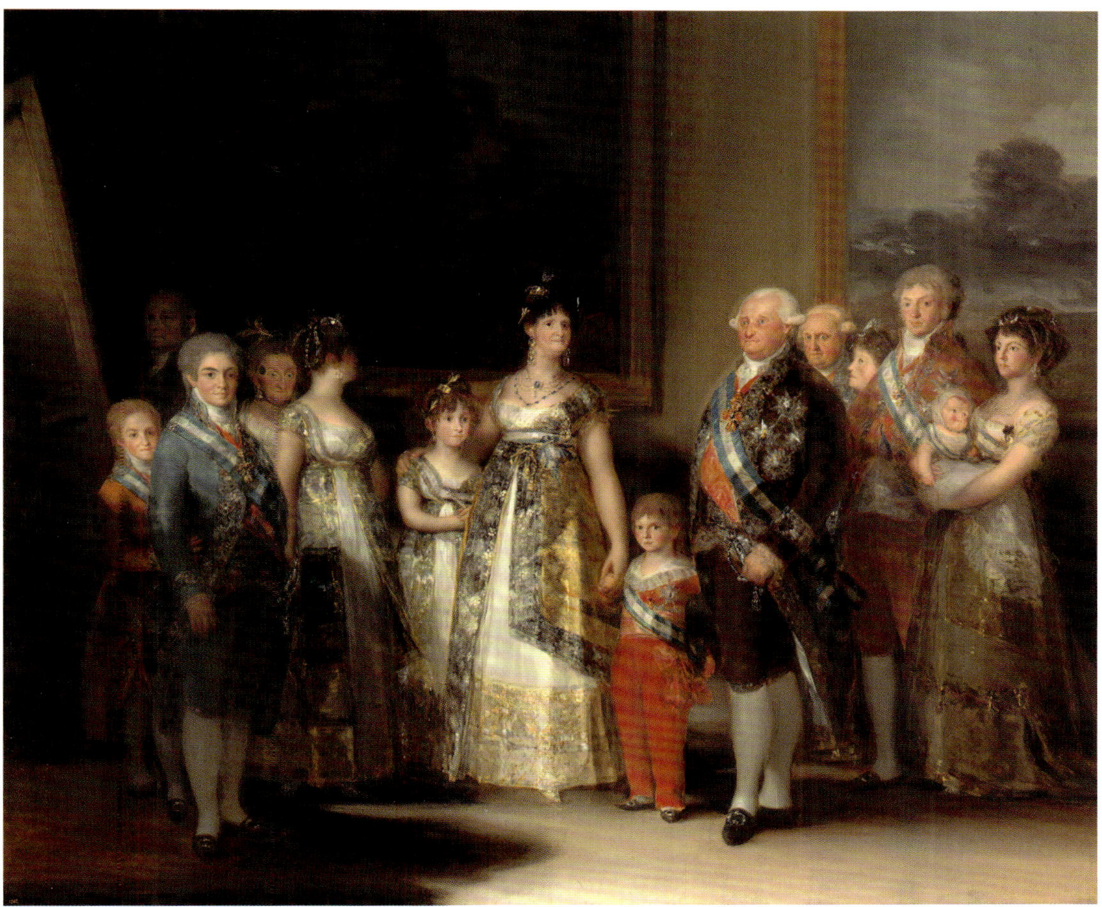

of Toledo. Goya's role as royal painter developed further, and, in October 1799, he became first court painter. In 1800, he painted what was to be his most substantial commission for a royal portrait, a large canvas depicting King Carlos IV (1748–1819) and his family (fig. 4), the most significant royal portrait in Spain after Velázquez's *Las Meninas*.

Spain was among the European countries deeply shaken by the political and social changes that resulted from the outbreak of the French Revolution in 1789 and the subsequent ascent of Napoleon Bonaparte (1769–1821). In 1808, Carlos IV abdicated, and Napoleon's brother, Joseph Bonaparte (1768–1844), ascended the throne of Spain as King José I. For six years, between 1808 and 1814, Spain was convulsed by the so-called Peninsular War, fought between Spanish resistance forces, Portugal, and the United

Fig. 3
Francisco de Goya y Lucientes
The Duchess of Alba, 1797
Oil on canvas, 82¹³⁄₁₆ × 58¾ in.
(210.3 × 149.3 cm)
The Hispanic Society of America, New York

Fig. 4
Francisco de Goya y Lucientes
The Family of King Carlos IV of Spain, 1800
Oil on canvas
110¼ × 132¼ in. (280 × 336 cm)
Museo Nacional del Prado, Madrid

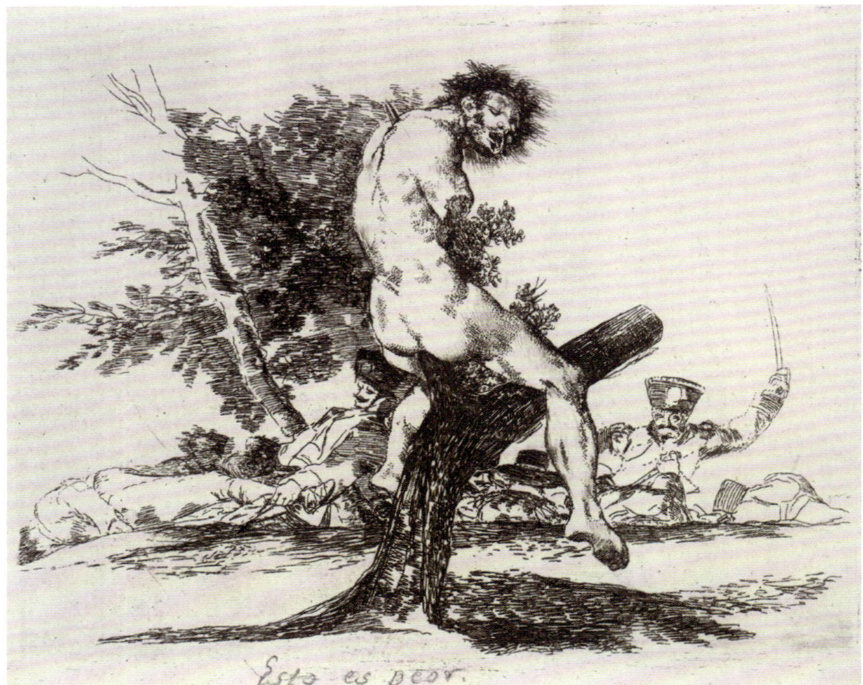

Fig. 5
Francisco de Goya y Lucientes
This Is Worse (*Esto es peor*), plate
37 from *The Disasters of War* (*Los
desastres de la guerra*), 1810 (first
published 1863)
Etching, lavis, and drypoint on
paper
6⅛ × 8⅝ in. (155 × 205 mm)
The British Museum, London

Kingdom against the French invaders; in Spain, this war was known as the War of Independence. This was a difficult time for Goya, as it was for the entire Spanish population. Between 1810 and 1815, Goya worked on *The Disasters of War* (*Los desastres de la guerra*), a set of eighty-two prints that depict the horrors of war but was not, in fact, published until 1863, thirty-five years after the painter's death. The extraordinary creation of a deaf painter surrounded by senseless violence, the *Disasters* (fig. 5) remains, to this day, one of the most harrowing portrayals of human cruelty. The tragedy of the war period was compounded for Goya by the loss of his wife Josefa, who died on June 20, 1812.

In June 1813, Joseph Bonaparte left Spain for the last time, and the son of King Carlos IV—Fernando VII (1784–1833)—assumed the Crown of Spain. That year, inspired by the heroism of Spanish citizens in their resistance against the French, Goya painted two monumental canvases (figs. 6, 7) that depict the events that took place in Madrid on May 2 and 3 of 1808. On the morning of May 2, a group of citizens attacked French and Mamluk soldiers in the main square of Madrid—the Puerta del Sol—only to be rounded up later that day, brought to three locations in the city, and shot during the night. These two incidents became the quintessential images of the Peninsular War in the public imagination.

Around this time, in 1815, Goya depicted himself in a stirring self-portrait (page 10) that focuses on his head, slightly tilted to the right and looking out at the viewer. This image of the almost seventy-year-old painter, a survivor of one of the most turbulent times in his country's history, is probably chronologically closest to the painting of *The Forge*. The second half of the 1810s saw Goya at work on two important altarpieces. In 1817, he produced a large painting for the altar of one of the sacristies of the Cathedral of Seville, showing Justa and Rufina (fig. 8), the patron saints of the city. Justa and Rufina were sisters who were active as potters in the neighborhood of Triana in Seville, in the third century. Martyred for refusing to worship pagan idols, Justa died first, in prison. Rufina was thrown to lions in the city's amphitheater and then killed when the lions refused to attack her. Goya shows the sisters standing, holding earthenware pots they created and diminutive palms that symbolize their martyrdom. At the feet of Justa are pieces of a smashed statue of the goddess Venus, while a large lion licks Rufina's feet. Both saints look heavenward while in the background the Cathedral of Seville, with its bell tower, the Giralda, can be seen. Two years later, on May 9, 1819, Goya was commissioned by the Piarist Fathers of Madrid to create an even larger altarpiece—the *Last Communion of St. José de Calasanz* (fig. 9)—for their church of San Antón. The altarpiece was completed by September of that year. The Spaniard José de Calasanz (1557–1648) was the founder of the Piarist order, and he ran the Escuelas Pías (Pious Schools), educational institutions for indigent boys. Goya's prodigious canvas shows the saint at the end of his life, when, on August 1, 1648, he took Communion for the last time. In his priestly black outfit—his biretta to the side on the floor and his hands joined in prayer—Calasanz kneels on a red cushion. To the left stands a younger priest, wearing a chasuble bordered with gold, who is administering Communion to the saint. The scene is set in an ill-defined cavernous church, in the background of which—as a tragic chorus to the scene—are the Piarist fathers to the left and the children being educated by the Pious Schools on the right. With their muted tones, occasionally accented by bright colors (the red of Calasanz's cushion or the red and yellow of Justa's and Rufina's dresses), the color schemes of these two altarpieces and their general atmosphere are very similar to that of *The Forge*.

Following pages:

Fig. 6
Francisco de Goya y Lucientes
The 2nd of May 1808 in Madrid or *The Fight against the Mamluks*, 1814
Oil on canvas
105⅝ × 136⅞ in.
(268.5 × 347.5 cm)
Museo Nacional del Prado, Madrid

Fig. 7
Francisco de Goya y Lucientes
The 3rd of May 1808 in Madrid or *The Executions*, 1814
Oil on canvas
105½ × 136⅝ in. (268 × 347 cm)
Museo Nacional del Prado, Madrid

Fig. 8
Francisco de Goya y Lucientes
Sts. Justa and Rufina, 1817
Oil on canvas
121⅝ × 69⅝ in. (309 × 177 cm)
Cathedral, Seville

Fig. 9
Francisco de Goya y Lucientes
The Last Communion of St. José de Calasanz, 1819
Oil on canvas
120⅛ × 87⅜ in. (305 × 222 cm)
Iglesia Colegio Escolapios de San Antón, Madrid

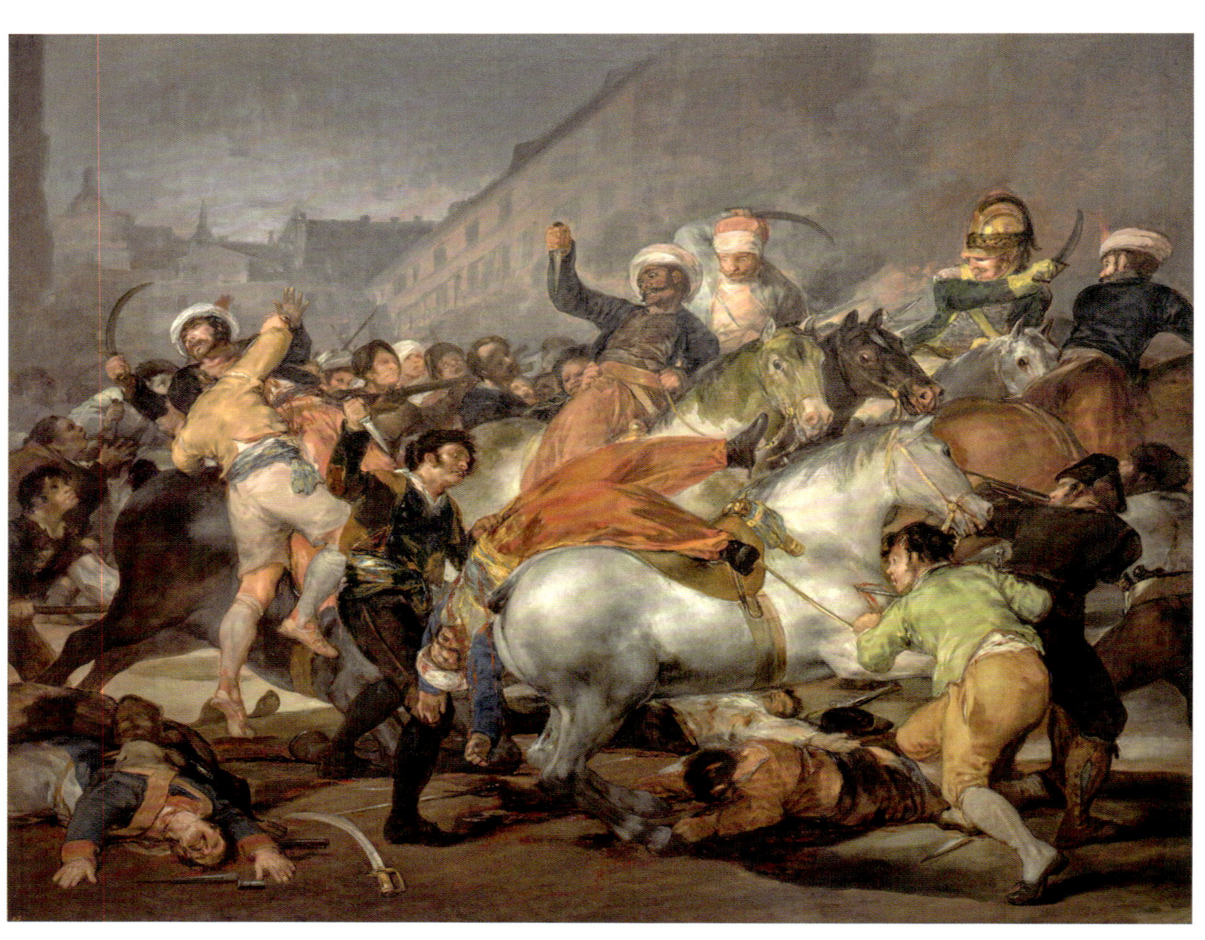

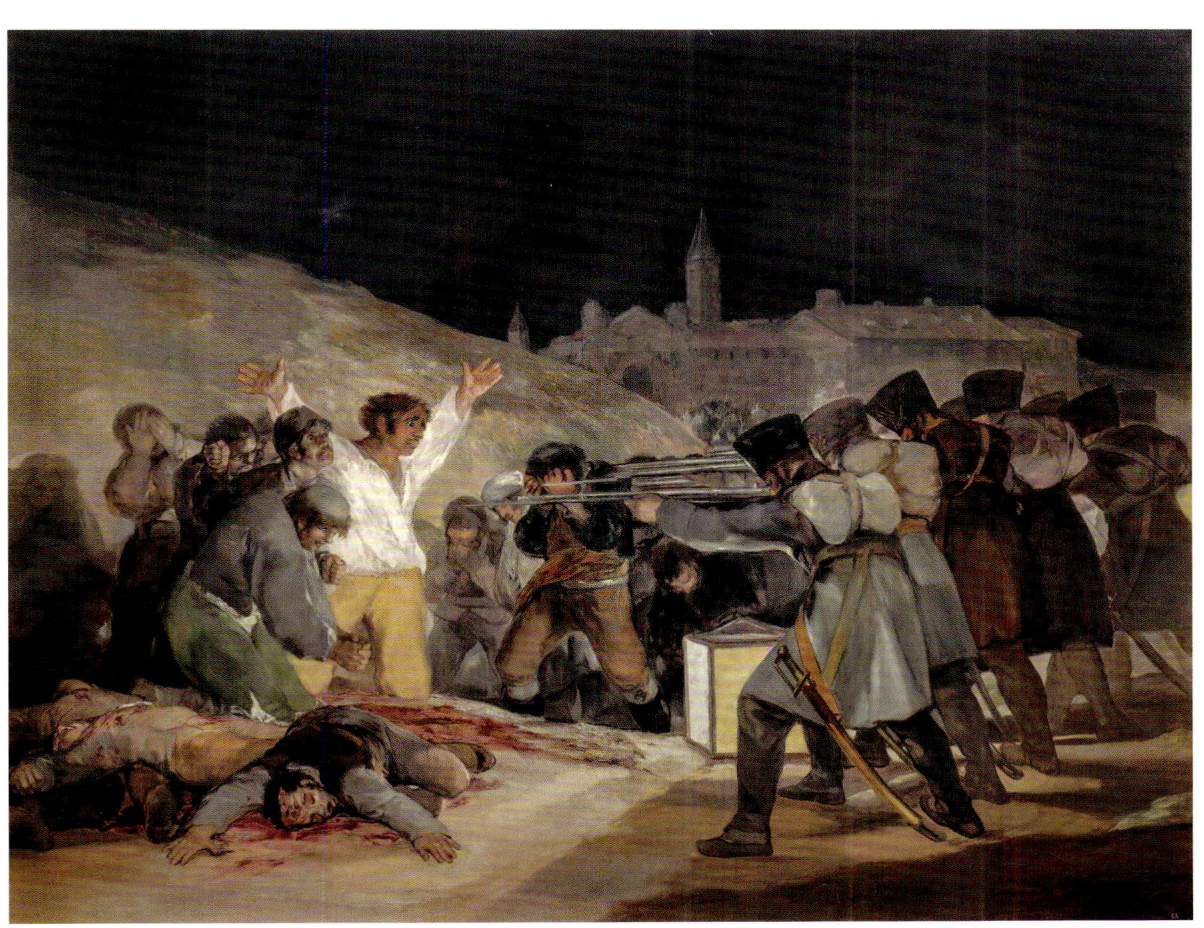

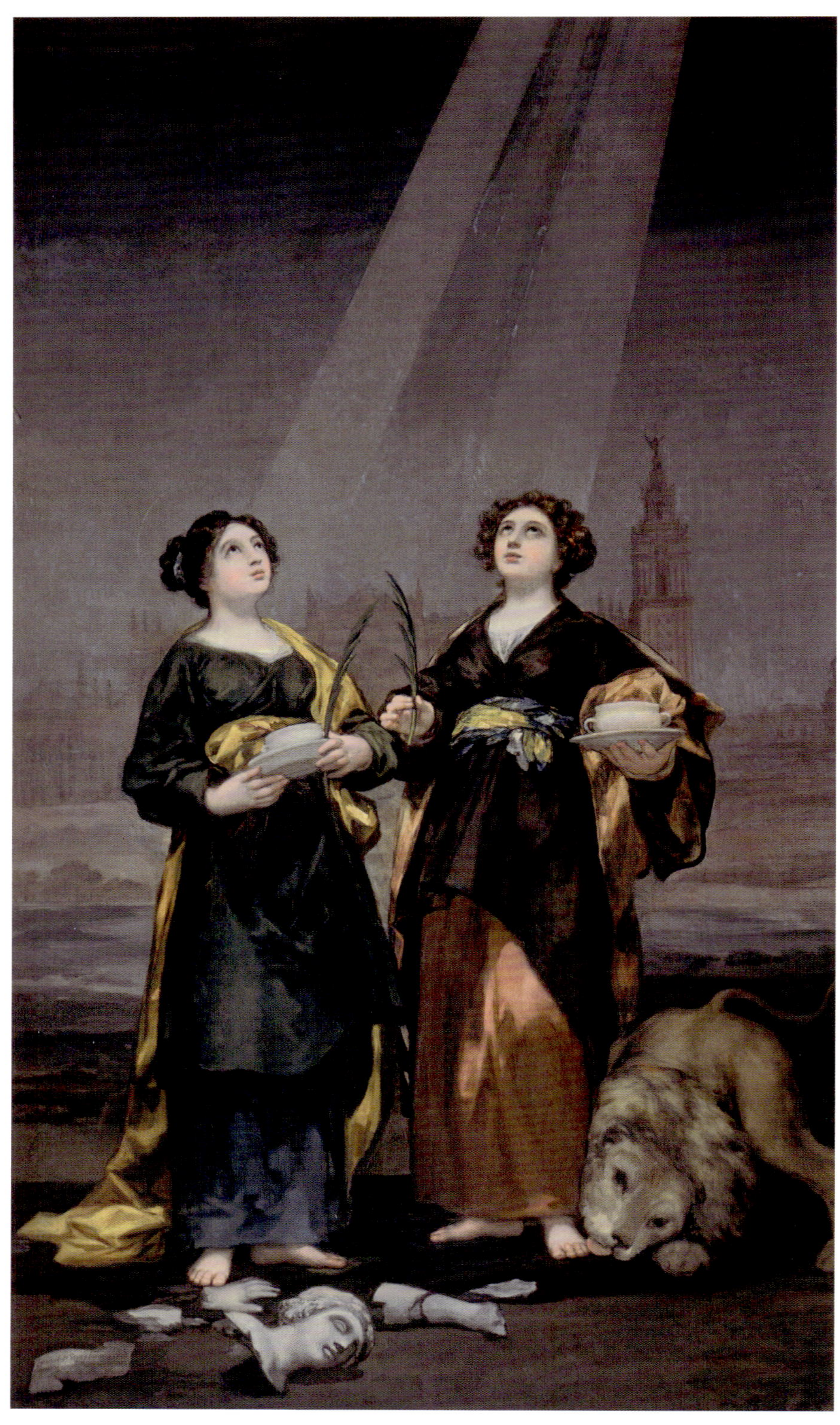

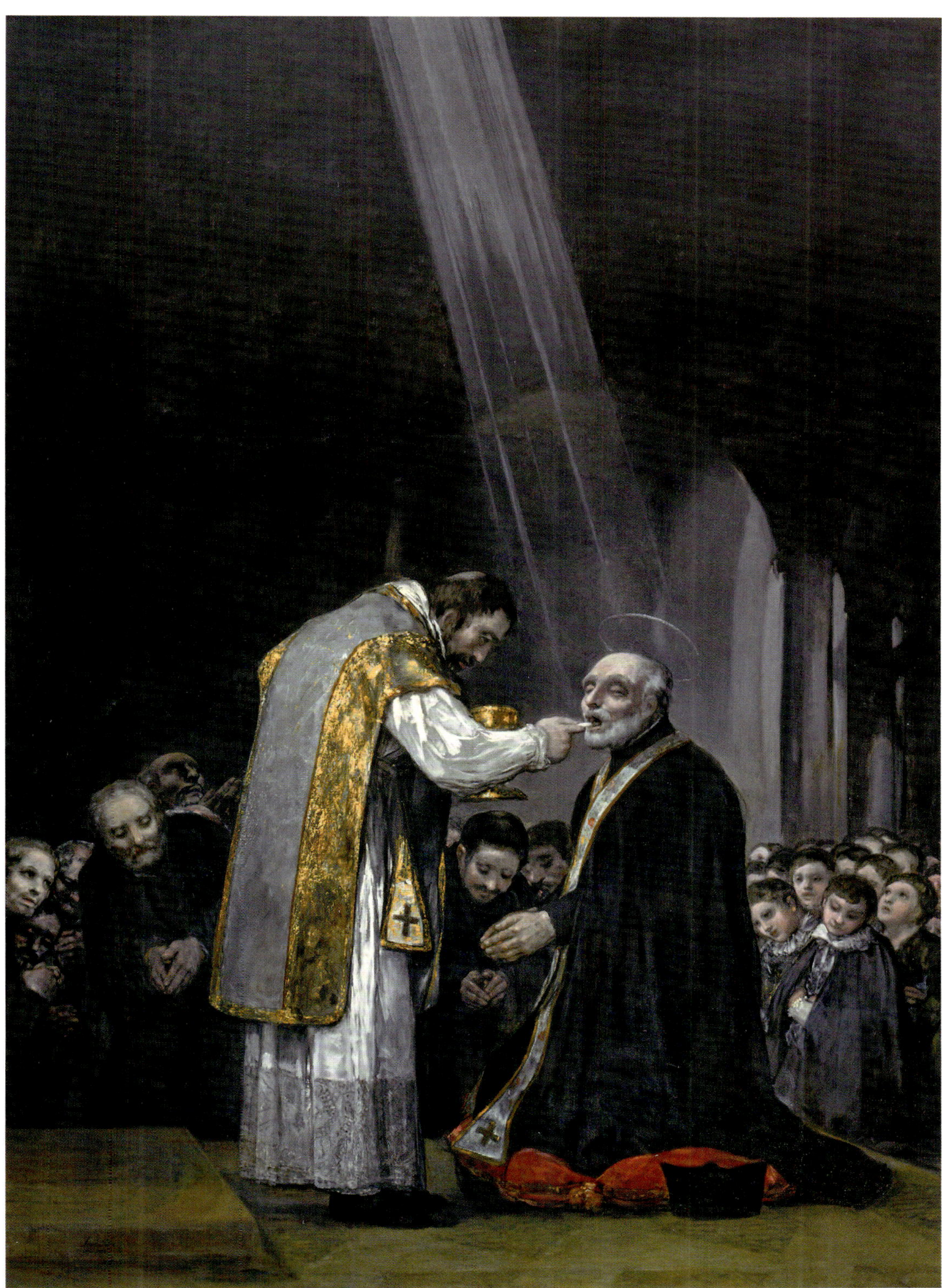

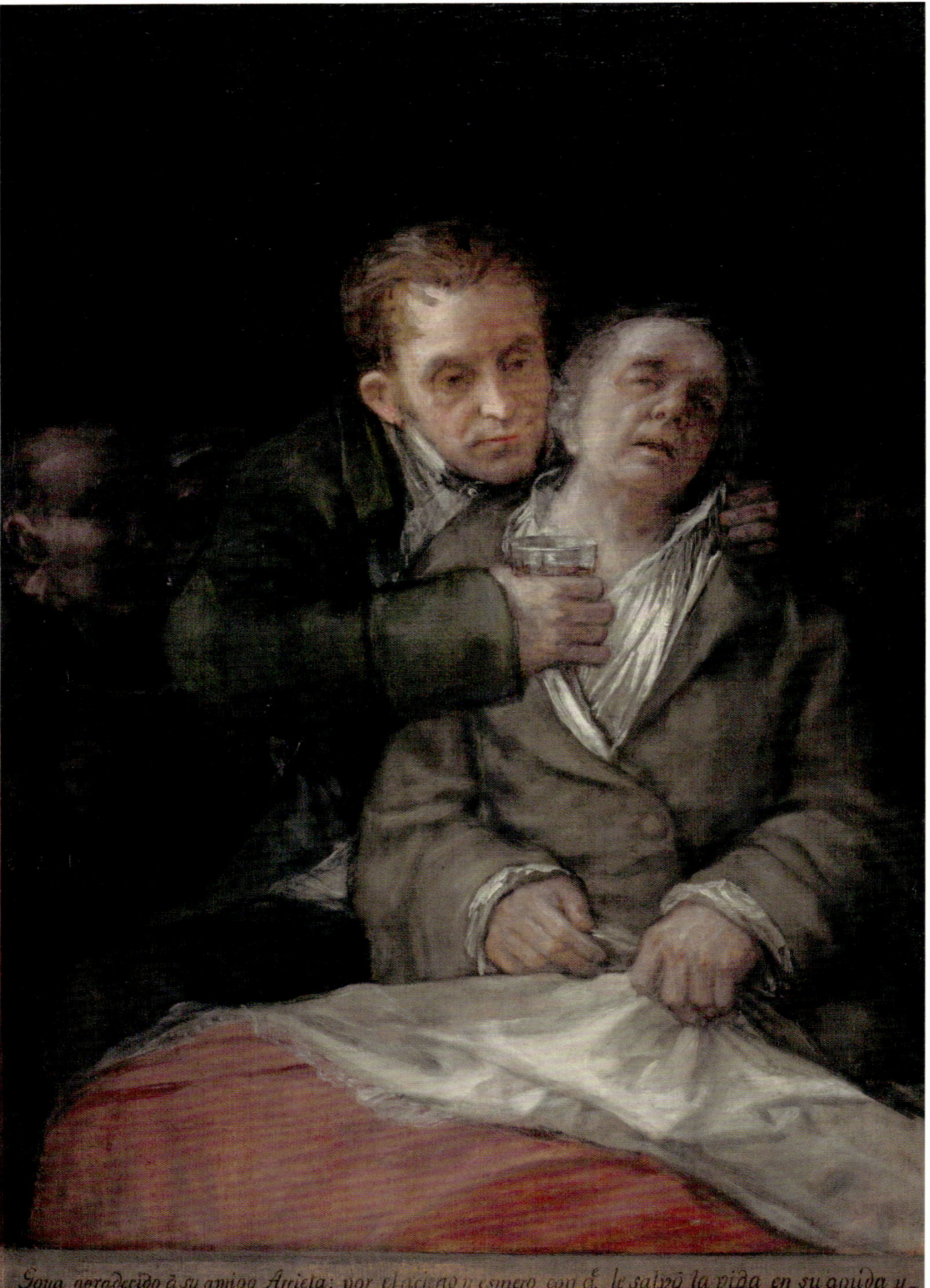

Goya agradecido, á su amigo Arrieta: por el acierto y esmero con q.^e le salvó la vida en su aguda y
peligrosa enfermedad, padecida á fines del año 1819, a los setenta y tres de su edad. Lo pintó en 1820.

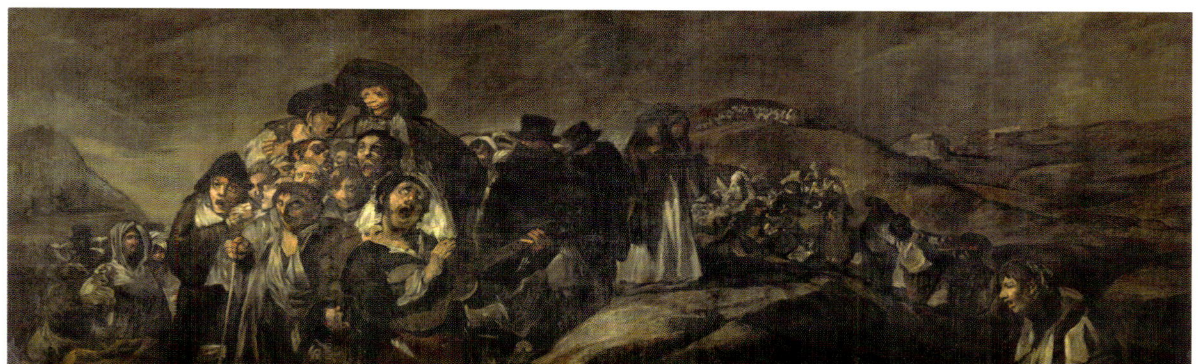

Goya became severely ill in 1819 but survived thanks to the ministrations of Dr. Eugenio García Arrieta. In gratitude to the doctor, the painter created an unusual self-portrait showing himself being attended to by Arrieta during his sickness (fig. 10). The early 1820s was a remarkably creative period in Goya's late life. In February 1819, he had acquired a small country house across the Manzanares River from the Royal Palace of Madrid. Coincidentally, the house was known as the Quinta del Sordo (Villa of the Deaf Man) because of a previous owner. Between 1820 and 1823, Goya decorated the walls of the house with a series of fourteen (possibly fifteen) murals. The two floors of the house were populated by Goya with scenes of curious subjects—some mythological, others genre and witchcraft scenes—in extremely dark tones, which gave the paintings the popular name of *Pinturas negras* (Black Paintings) (fig. 11). Any understanding of these paintings today is compromised by their poor state of conservation, following their being detached from the walls of the house in the 1870s, and by their separation from their original context (the house was demolished in 1909).

For the last four years of his life, Goya lived in France. In 1824, he traveled to Paris and later settled in Bordeaux, where he established himself, together with his companion, Leocadia Weiss (1788–1856). Goya's friend, the poet Leandro Fernández de Moratín (1760–1828), writing from Bordeaux on June 27, 1824, described how he "in fact arrived, deaf, old, awkward, and weak, and without knowing a word of French, and without a servant (that no one needs more than he), and so content and so desirous to see the world."[10] Working up to the last months of his life, Goya died in Bordeaux on April 16, 1828, at the age of eighty-two.

Fig. 10
Francisco de Goya y Lucientes
Self-Portrait with Dr. Arrieta,
1820
Oil on canvas
45 ⅛ × 30 ⅛ in. (114.6 × 76.5 cm)
Minneapolis Institute of Art,
Minneapolis

Fig. 11
Francisco de Goya y Lucientes
The Pilgrimage to San Isidro,
1820–23
Mural transferred to canvas
54 ½ × 171⅝ in.
(138.5 × 436 cm)
Museo Nacional del Prado,
Madrid

Fig. 12
Francisco de Goya y Lucientes
Maja and Celestina on a Balcony,
ca. 1808–12
Oil on canvas
65 ⅜ × 42 ½ in. (166 × 108 cm)
Private collection, Madrid

Creating *The Forge*

The Forge is first documented in 1836, eight years after Goya's death. Proposals for the date of its creation have shifted widely across the 1810s, based entirely on stylistic analysis. In December 1812, an inventory of the paintings in Goya's home, on the Calle de Valverde in Madrid, was compiled after the death of his wife Josefa, as part of a division of property between Goya and his son.[11] The paintings to be given to Javier were marked with large *X*'s in white paint followed by a number; these *X* numbers still survive on some of the canvases described in the inventory, while they were later removed from others. The 1812 inventory includes a number of impressive canvases of genre scenes—such as the *Majas on a Balcony* (now in a private collection in Switzerland) and the *Maja and Celestina on a Balcony* (fig. 12)—that were painted by Goya at the time of the Peninsular War. Technical analysis shows that these works were all created on reused canvases, no doubt due to the lack of available materials during the war.[12] Another painting by Goya described in the 1812 inventory is the *Lazarillo de Tormes* (fig. 13), which illustrates an episode from the sixteenth-century picaresque novel of the same name that centers on a poor young boy, Lazarillo, who serves as an apprentice to a blind beggar. Lazarillo's cunning is central to the text, and, in the episode depicted by Goya, the blind beggar is searching the young boy's mouth after he has stolen a sausage from him, the man placing his nose close to Lazarillo's mouth. The crude scene is depicted by Goya as a close-up of the two figures. Set by a fire—visible in the right-hand corner—the beggar and Lazarillo are humbly dressed. In terms of style and color scheme, the work is similar to *The Forge*. As *The Forge* does not appear in the inventory, and as it was painted on a new canvas, it is generally agreed that the painting must postdate the 1812 inventory and the war.[13] Some scholars believe *The Forge* postdates the 1812 inventory by only a few years and should be dated somewhere between 1813 and 1815, making it contemporary with the large canvases showing the events of May 2 and 3 of 1808 (see figs. 6, 7).[14] Others maintain that *The Forge* dates from the early 1820s, "at the same time as the 'Black Pictures,' or very little earlier."[15] There seems to be a consensus around a compromise between these two positions, with most scholars, as well as the most recent literature, dating *The Forge* between 1815 and 1820.[16] During the 1810s, Goya's style developed in different directions, and while it is true that a painting like *The Forge* has much in common with pictures such as the

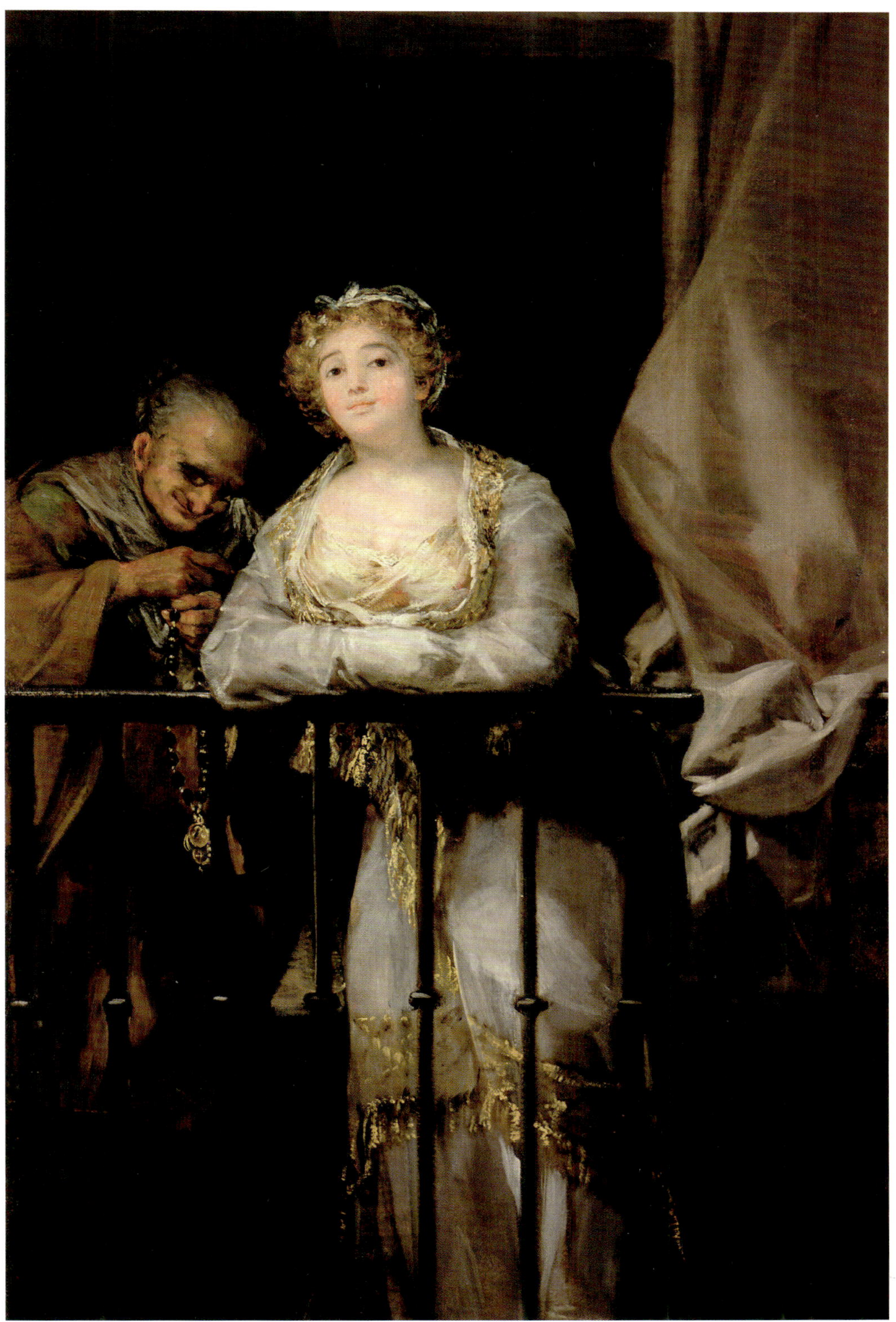

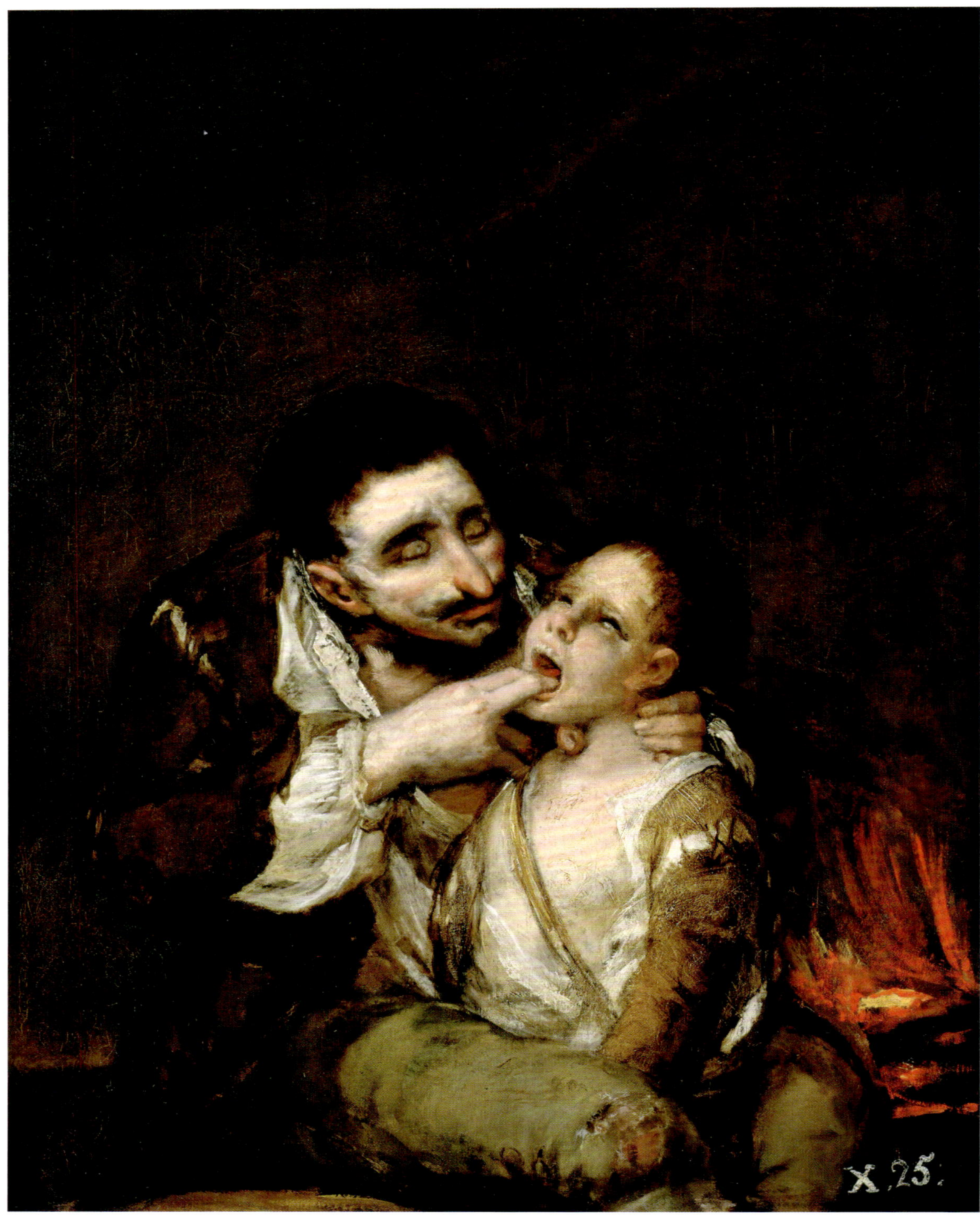

X, 25.

Lazarillo de Tormes, which must have been painted before 1812, at the time of the war, it also has many stylistic similarities with paintings created at the end of that decade, such as the *Last Communion of St. José de Calasanz* (see fig. 9). Furthermore, the fact that *The Forge* does not appear in the 1812 inventory does not preclude its existence by that date; the inventory only lists pictures that were in Goya's possession by that date. *The Forge* could have been sold before 1812, in which case it would not have appeared on that list. On the other hand, the fact that Goya used a new canvas for *The Forge* seems to suggest that the picture was indeed painted after the end of the war, in 1814. It is simply not possible to provide an exact date for the painting; placing it somewhere between the conclusion of the Peninsular War and the painting of the murals in the Quinta del Sordo is the most reasonable conclusion.

Deciphering the meaning of *The Forge* is as difficult as dating it. When Goya helped compile the inventory of the royal collection in February 1794, one of the most highly valued paintings, at 60,000 *reales*, was Velázquez's magnificent *Forge of Vulcan* (fig. 14).[17] Painted in 1630, during the first of Velázquez's two trips to Italy, the large painting depicts a mythological scene. In resplendent orange drapery and wearing a laurel wreath, the god Apollo enters the forge of Vulcan, where, together with his assistants, he is creating armor for his fellow gods. Apollo has come to inform Vulcan that his wife, Venus, is having an affair with another god, Mars, news that stuns Vulcan and his companions. Velázquez depicts Apollo in a classical robe, while Vulcan and his assistants are covered, in the heat of the forge, only by small loincloths. While the scene is intended to represent a mythological episode, Velázquez depicts Vulcan and his assistants in a contemporary forge. The fireplace to the right, the anvils, tools, and armor would all have been instantly recognizable as contemporary objects by a seventeenth-century viewer. Goya clearly knew the painting well, and his own *Forge*, painted almost two hundred years later, is deeply indebted to the Velázquez canvas. It is as if Goya condensed three of the figures from Velázquez's *Forge of Vulcan* into his own version of the painting. Velázquez's Vulcan, standing by the anvil and holding on it a piece of molten metal, is transformed by Goya into the young man on the left leaning over the anvil and holding down the piece of metal. The man at the far right in Velázquez's painting, cutting another piece of metal, is brought by Goya closer to the anvil, operating bellows. The man in a brown loincloth at the center of Velázquez's forge shares three features with the central figure in Goya's *Forge*.

Fig. 13
Francisco de Goya y Lucientes
Lazarillo de Tormes, ca. 1808–12
Oil on canvas
31½ × 25⁹⁄₁₆ in. (80 × 65 cm)
Private collection, Madrid

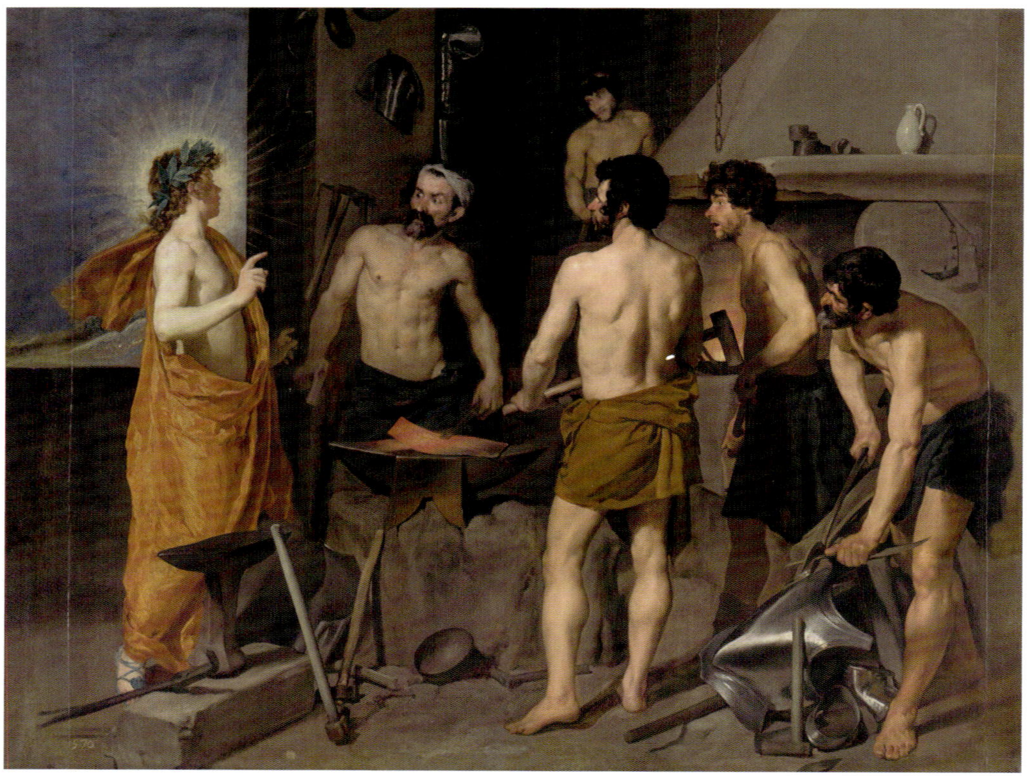

Fig. 14
Diego Rodríguez de Silva y
Velázquez
The Forge of Vulcan, 1630
Oil on canvas
87⅞ × 114¼ in. (223 × 290 cm)
Museo Nacional del Prado,
Madrid

The left calves of both figures are prominently displayed, as are their muscular backs, nude in the case of Velázquez, covered by the white shirt but fully legible in Goya's version; and they hold the same sledgehammer. It is as if Goya captured the moment either immediately preceding the arrival, or following the departure, of Apollo. Of course, Goya is not depicting a mythological subject, and the contemporary costume in his *Forge* indicates that the painting was not meant to represent the forge of Vulcan. The mythological subject, derived from Ovid's *Metamorphoses*, was commonly depicted in sixteenth- and seventeenth-century paintings. Jacopo Tintoretto (1518–1594), for example, painted the *Forge of Vulcan* (fig. 15) in one of his four paintings for the Atrio Quadrato (now in the Sala dell'Anticollegio) in the Doge's Palace in Venice.[18] As in Goya's canvas, the Tintoretto painting also centers on a figure seen from the back and lifting a sledgehammer; the figure holding the sheet of metal down on the anvil is also similar. Luca Giordano painted a *Forge of Vulcan* (fig. 16), which, in its claustrophobic close-up, recalls Goya's solution.

The Forge is clearly indebted to the long-standing tradition of representing the mythological forges of Vulcan, but, by depicting a contemporary blacksmith's shop, Goya transformed a classical, mythological scene into a genre picture. Throughout the late eighteenth and nineteenth centuries, painters such as Joseph Wright of Derby (1734–1797; fig. 17), Théodore Géricault (1791–1824), and Honoré Daumier (1808–1879) painted contemporary scenes of blacksmiths and forges.[19] According to Jane Kristof, the blacksmith at the time "became a kind of symbol of the worker's resistance to urbanization."[20] While this reading surely applies to paintings produced in England and France at a time of industrial development, it is less likely that such an interpretation would be relevant to a picture created in Spain after the Peninsular War.

Other scholars have attached a more complex meaning to *The Forge*, arguing that it could refer to French revolutionary allegorical prints showing three men—representing the aristocracy, the clergy, and the common man— hammering at an anvil as a representation of the creation of the 1791 French

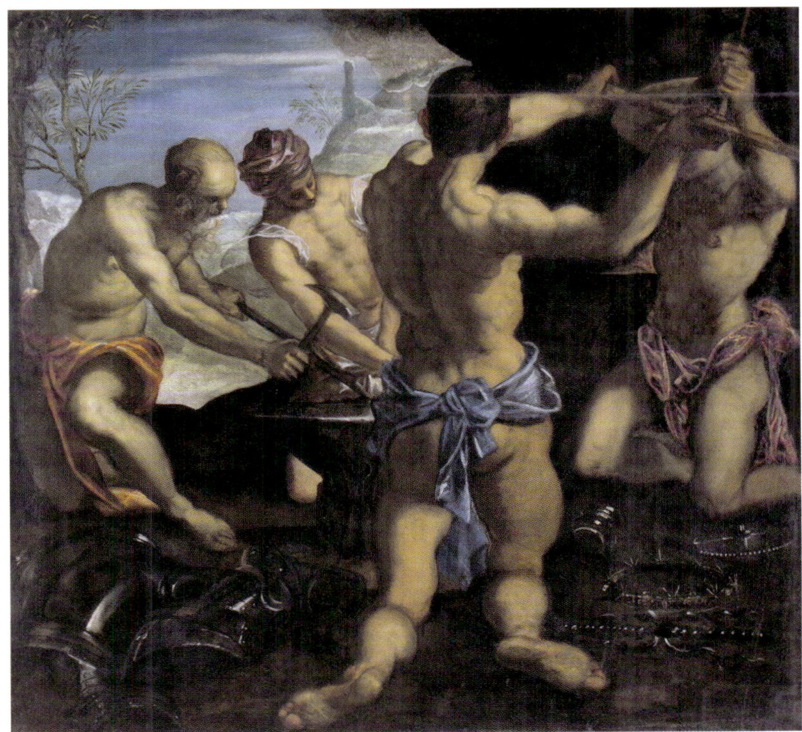

Fig. 15
Jacopo Tintoretto
The Forge of Vulcan, 1576–78
Oil on canvas
98½ × 70⅞ in. (250 × 180 cm)
Doge's Palace, Venice

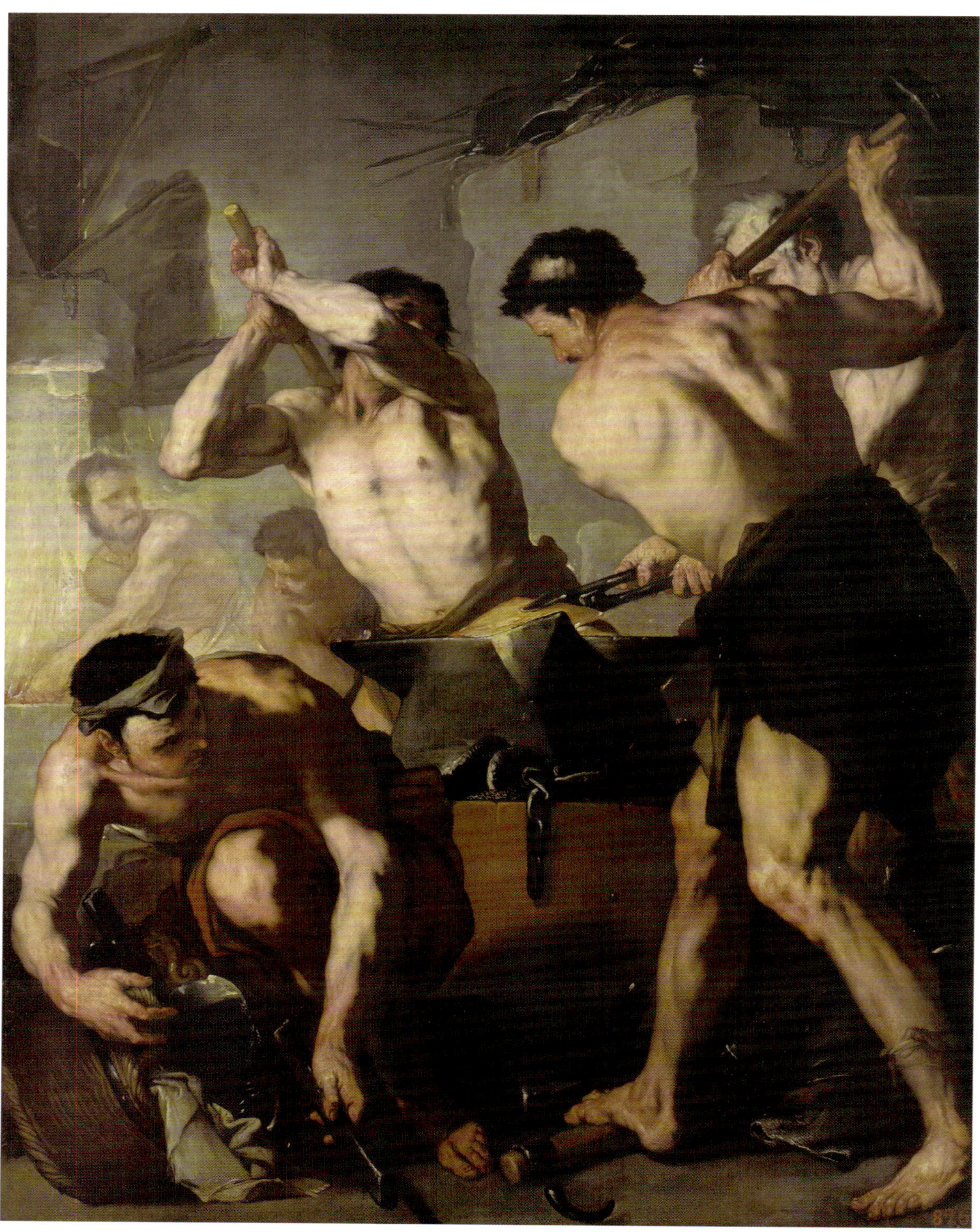

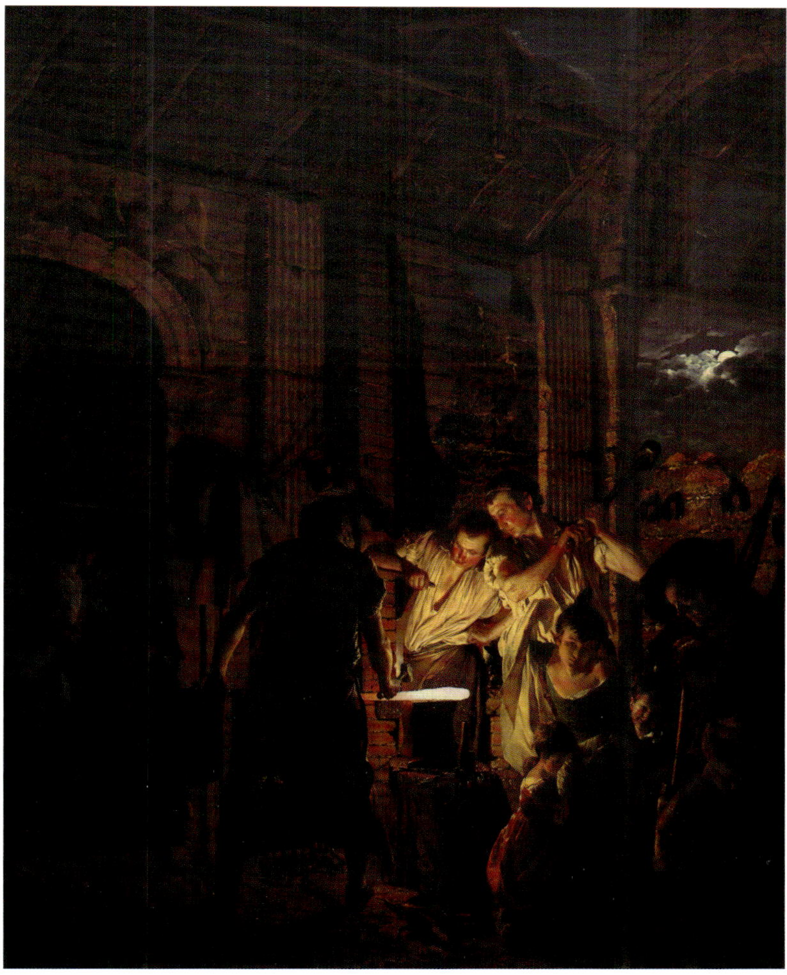

Fig. 16
Luca Giordano
The Forge of Vulcan, ca. 1660
Oil on canvas
75⅞ × 59⅝ in.
(192.5 × 151.5 cm)
The State Hermitage Museum,
St. Petersburg

Fig. 17
Joseph Wright of Derby
The Blacksmith's Shop, 1771
Oil on canvas
49½ × 39 in. (125.7 × 99 cm)
Derby Museum and Art Gallery,
Derby

constitution. Goya's *Forge* "perhaps refers to their participation in the making of" the Spanish Constitution of 1812;[21] more generally, the three men in *The Forge* can be seen as "representatives of the *pueblo*, hammering out Spain's future—to use a common phrase of the day, which may have supplied Goya with the allegorical dimension of his painting—on the anvil of its history."[22] As tempting as such readings might be, there is no evidence that Goya planned to represent anything in the canvas beyond smiths in a forge. Examples of such straightforward genre scenes that predate Goya include an elegant painting by one of the Le Nain brothers, from around 1640, showing a blacksmith working in his forge, surrounded by his father, wife, and children (fig. 18).

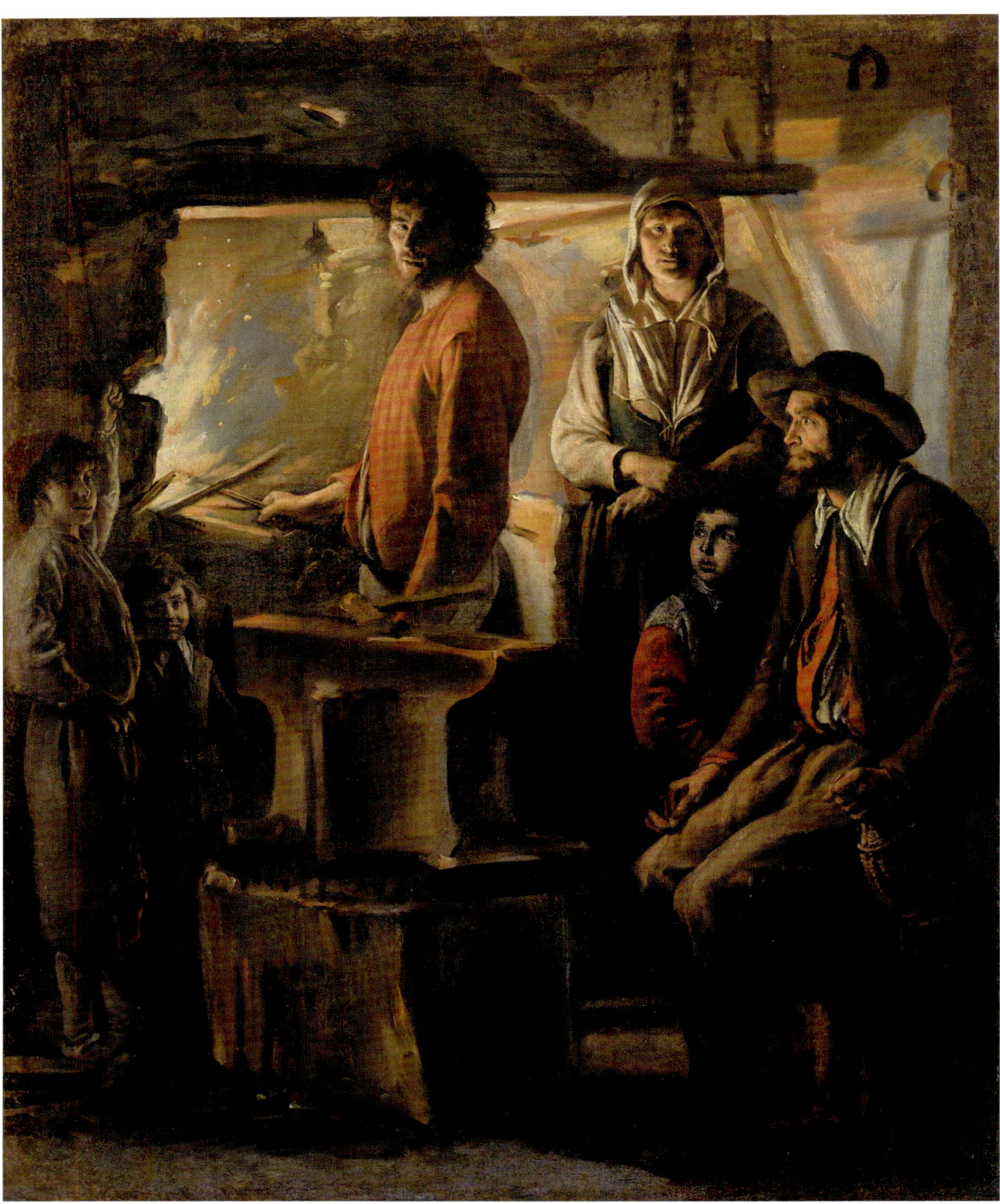

Admittedly, the small scale of Le Nain's picture is appropriate for a genre scene, while the large scale that Goya chose for his scene relates to mythological and allegorical subjects.

Two other works by Goya from the 1810s are closely associated with *The Forge*. Among the prints of the *Disasters of War*, a sheet of extreme violence titled *The Same* (*Lo mismo*) (fig. 19) shows a Spanish man wielding a large axe over a group of French soldiers while a companion, to the left, climbs over the back of another soldier and stabs him. Formally, the man with the axe is analogous to the smith in *The Forge*. They are dressed similarly, with the rolled-up sleeves of the white shirt and the sock on the left leg slipping to reveal the calf; and the action of lifting the axe is almost identical, though taken from a different point of view to the lifting of the sledgehammer in *The Forge*. *The Same* is no doubt an earlier composition that Goya must have recalled when creating the later painting. Even more direct is the relationship between *The Forge* and a drawing believed to represent gravediggers (fig. 20) from Goya's so-called Album F, a sketchbook also known as the Sepia Album or the Images of Spain Album. Probably also created between 1812 and 1820, the drawings in the sketchbook are in ink and wash and represent single figures or groups, with little definition to provide settings or backgrounds.[23] The gravedigger drawing portrays three men standing on a pile of soil and digging into it. The figures are identical to those in *The Forge*, except that instead of working around an anvil, they are digging a hole in the ground. Instead of tongs and a sledgehammer, they are using hoes.[24] The drawing has been seen as "a first idea" for *The Forge*.[25] It is possible that Goya observed a group of men digging (possibly a grave), captured them in his sketchbook, and later, in his studio, used that drawing to transfer the figures into an interior and transform them into men at work in a forge. There is, however, no substantiation of this orderly sequence. It is equally possible that the drawing follows the painting and that Goya, for some reason, decided to take inspiration from *The Forge* to depict a group of men digging.[26] The drawing and painting are unquestionably linked, but the sequence of their creation and their exact relationship remains unknown.

The dating and meaning of *The Forge* is related to the purpose for which it was created, and that also remains unexplained. A large canvas of this kind would have most likely been painted with a specific purpose in mind. Fred Licht proposed in 1973 that:

Fig. 18
Antoine or Louis Le Nain
The Forge, ca. 1640
Oil on canvas
27¼ × 22⁷⁄₁₆ in. (69 × 57 cm)
Musée du Louvre, Paris

Fig. 19
Francisco de Goya y Lucientes
The Same (*Lo mismo*), plate 3
from *The Disasters of War* (*Los
desastres de la guerra*), 1810 (first
published 1863)
Etching, lavis, drypoint on paper
6¼ × 8⅝ in. (160 × 219 mm)
The British Museum, London

Fig. 20
Francisco de Goya y Lucientes
Three Men Digging, folio 51 from
Album F, ca. 1812–20
Brush, with brown and gray-
brown on laid paper
8⅛ × 5⅝ in. (206 × 143 mm)
The Metropolitan Museum of
Art, New York

Following pages:

Fig. 21
Francisco de Goya y Lucientes
Knife-Grinder, ca. 1808–12
Oil on canvas
26¾ × 19⅞ in. (68 × 50.5 cm)
Szépművészeti Múzeum,
Budapest

Fig. 22
Francisco de Goya y Lucientes
Water-Seller, ca 1808–12
Oil on canvas
26¾ × 19⅞ in. (68 × 50.5 cm)
Szépművészeti Múzeum,
Budapest

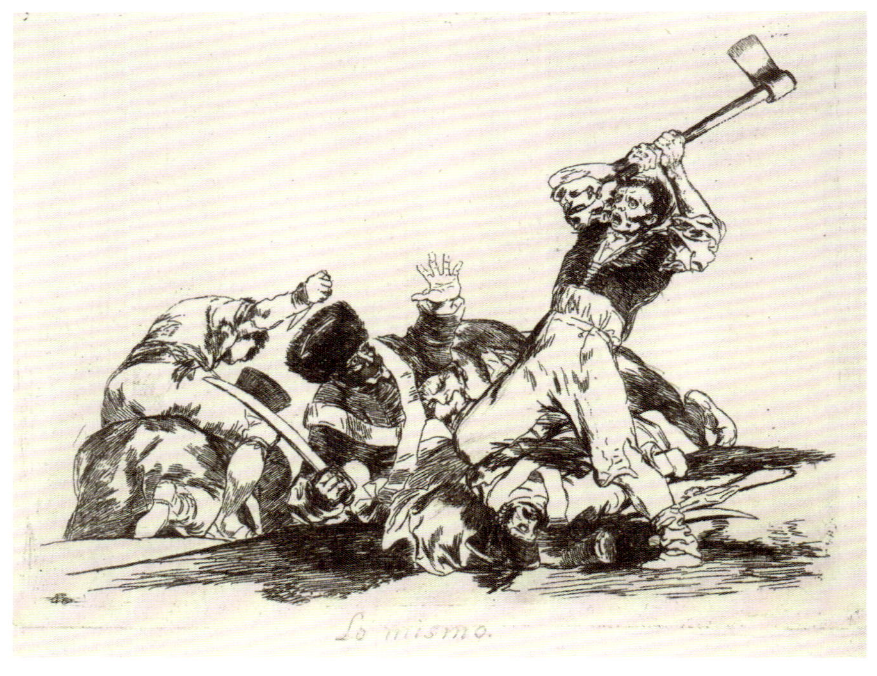

The Forge . . . must have been a commissioned work. It is unlike Goya, who had a shrewd and canny business sense, to paint so large and ambitious a canvas without receiving a commission and a decent advance payment for it. . . . Who could have commissioned such a painting in the first quarter of the nineteenth century? Even in the unlikely event that the painting wasn't commissioned, how could Goya have hoped to sell a picture such as this?[27]

In the early 1810s, Goya had painted two other images of working people, which were apparently not commissioned. Two pendant paintings, the *Knife-Grinder* (fig. 21) and the *Water-Seller* (fig. 22), depict human figures set against neutral backgrounds like *The Forge*.[28] In the first of the paintings, a man with his sleeves rolled up kneels over his portable wheel as he sharpens a knife. His attire is almost identical to that of the smith at the center of *The Forge*. In the companion painting, a woman carries a jug of water in one hand and a basket of glasses in the other. The idea put forth that the *Knife-Grinder* and *Water-Seller* represent the heroism of the Spanish people during the war is altogether unconvincing.[29] By 1812, both paintings were still in Goya's home and listed in the inventory of December of that year. They were painted

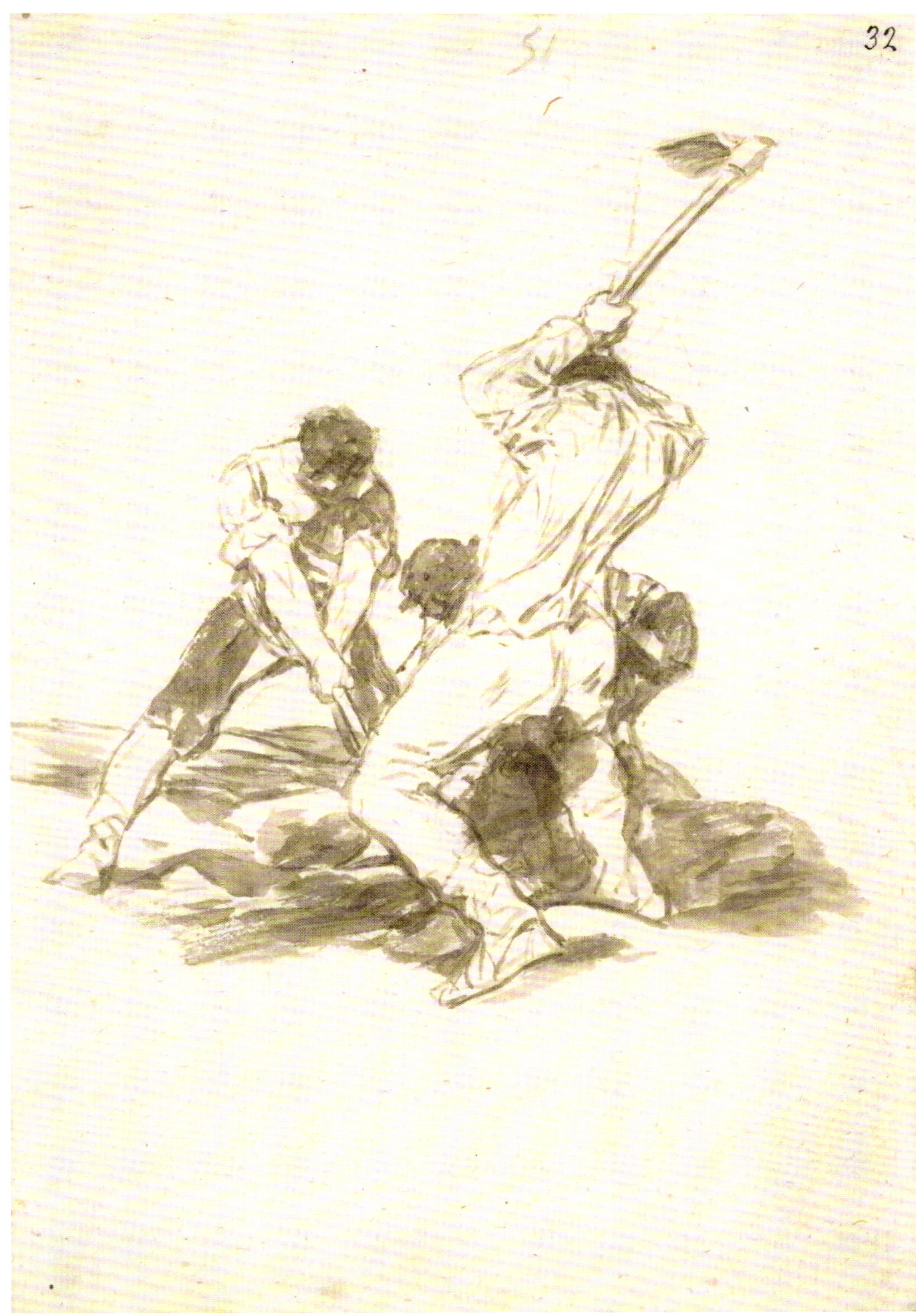

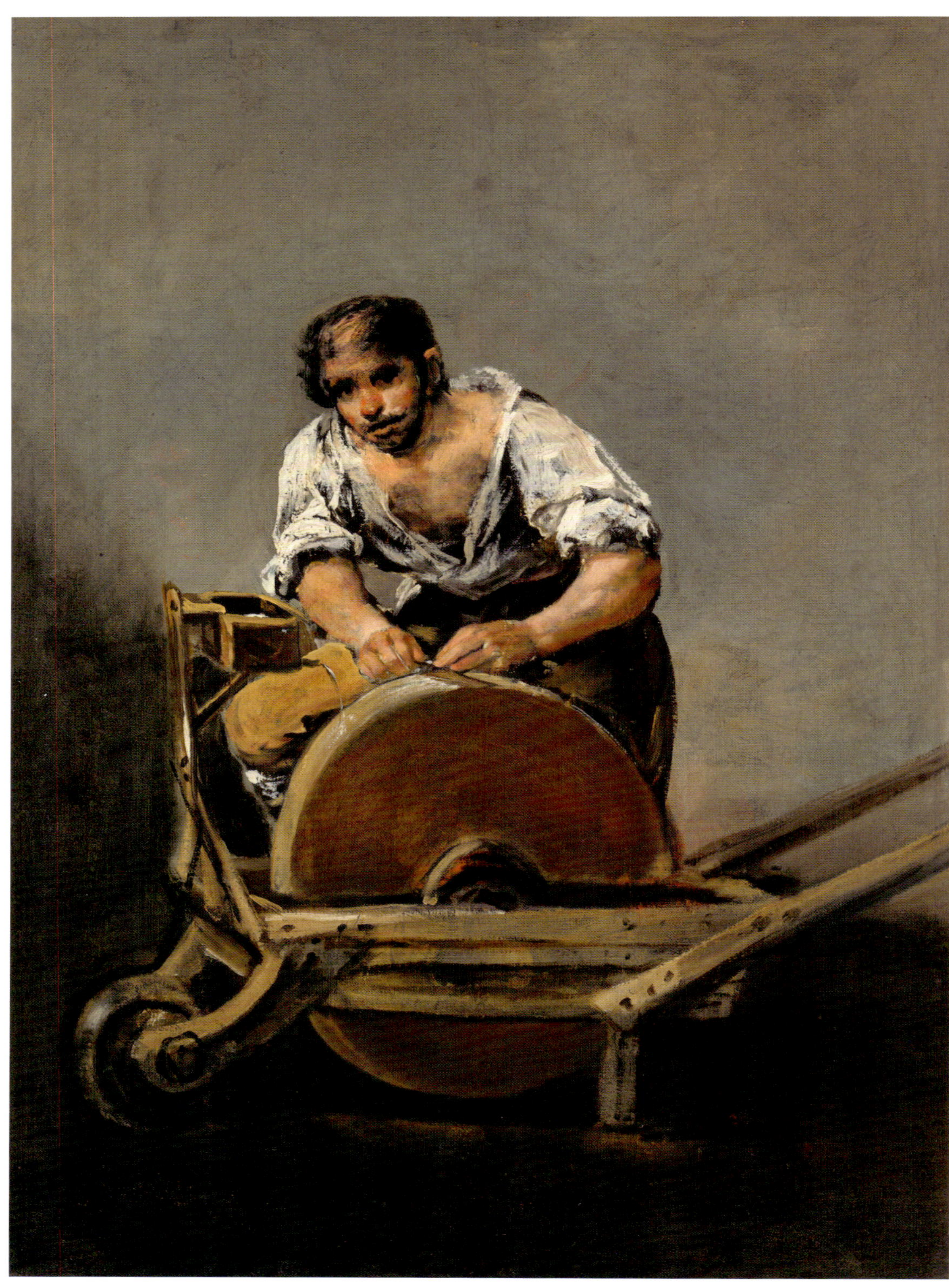

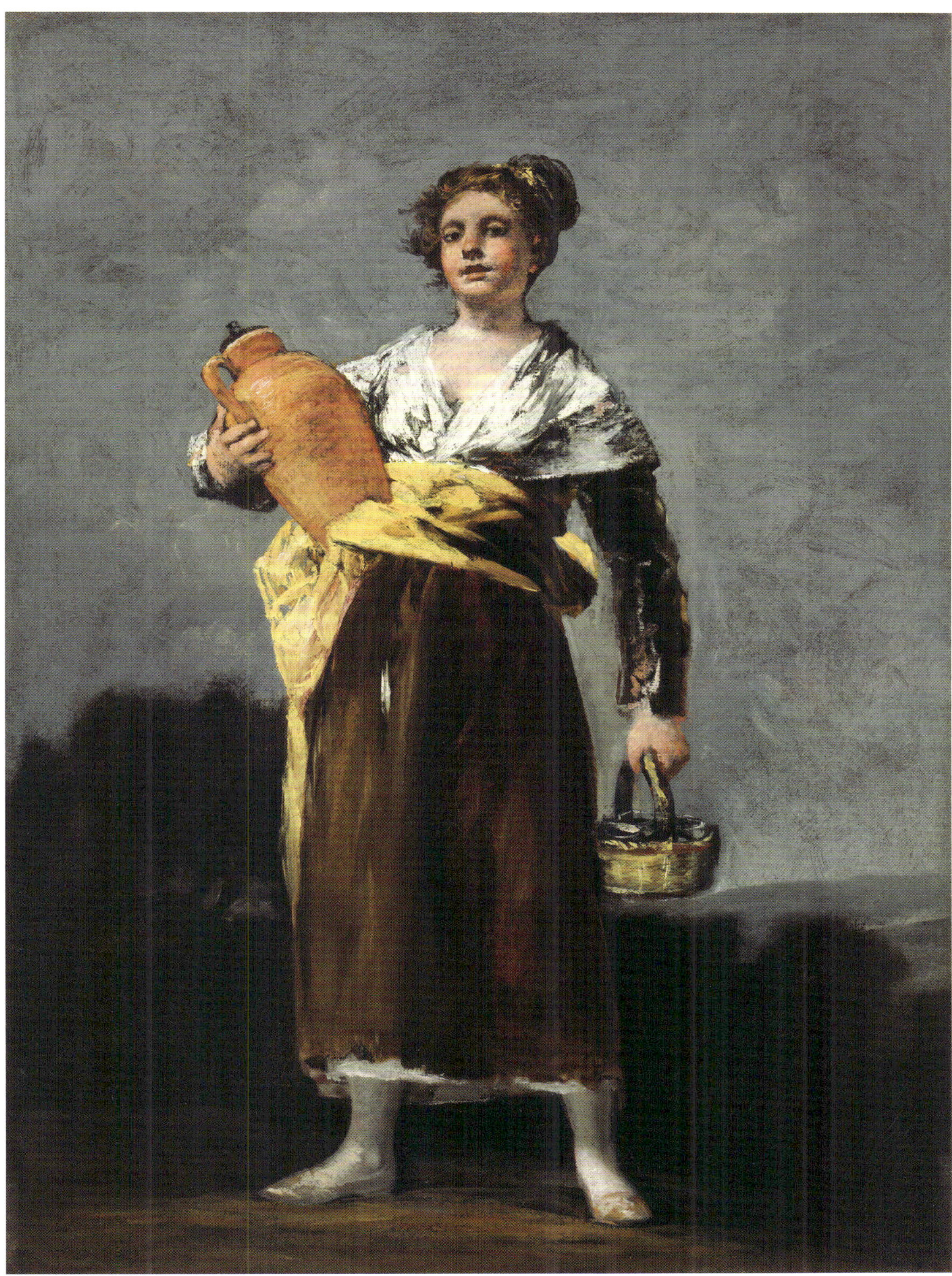

Fig. 23
Francisco de Goya y Lucientes
The Young Women (*Les Jeunes*) or
The Letter (*La Lettre*), ca. 1812–20
Oil on canvas
71¼ × 49¼ in. (181 × 125 cm)
Palais des Beaux-Arts, Lille

during the war, as proven by the canvases of the paintings, both of which had been reused—X-rays have revealed bouquets of flowers painted underneath them. As early as 1941, it was suggested that in the 1810s Goya intended to create a group of paintings representing tradespeople in Spain.[30] In subject matter, *The Forge* is most closely linked to the *Knife-Grinder* and *Water-Seller*, and this had been commented on in the literature on the paintings.[31] The idea, however, that Goya "planned at this time a series of large compositions depicting contemporary life, as a sort of parallel to the more sanguine attitude of the tapestry cartoons of so many years before" and that paintings such as the *Knife-Grinder* and the *Water-Seller*—but also the *Majas on a Balcony*, the *Maja and Celestina on a Balcony*, and other paintings that are described in the 1812 inventory—were part of a set is disproved by the different sizes of all these paintings.[32] *The Forge* is almost three times larger than the *Knife-Grinder* and the *Water-Seller*, which were painted on canvases much more appropriate for their genre subject matter.

The Early Provenance of *The Forge*

Louis-Philippe of Orléans (1773–1850) became king of the French in July 1830. Even as a young man, he had a particular fondness for Spain and Spanish art. As king, he entrusted the half-English, half-Belgian Isidore-Justin-Séverin, Baron Taylor (1789–1879), with a "scholarly mission" to travel to Spain to acquire paintings for France.[33] Between October 1835 and April 1837, Taylor collected about 440 Spanish paintings, mostly of the seventeenth and eighteenth centuries, in Castile and Andalusia.[34] Beginning on January 7, 1838, the paintings were put on public display in five rooms in the Louvre's Galeries de la Colonnade, which became known as the Galerie Espagnole or Musée Espagnol.[35] The king spent the enormous amount of 1.3 million francs on the enterprise. Among these works were eleven paintings by (or attributed to) Goya, including *The Forge*.[36] Taylor had bought *The Forge* in Madrid, on August 30, 1836, from Goya's son, Javier, together with another seven works by the painter, for the sum of 15,500 *reales*.[37] This 1836 date, after Goya's death, marks the first documented mention of *The Forge*.

We do not know where Goya's *Forge* was between its creation and 1836 and exactly when it belonged to Javier Goya. One clue, however, suggests that the painting was in a previous collection, the identity of which is unknown. When *The Forge* was restored in 1954, an inscription in white paint was found in the

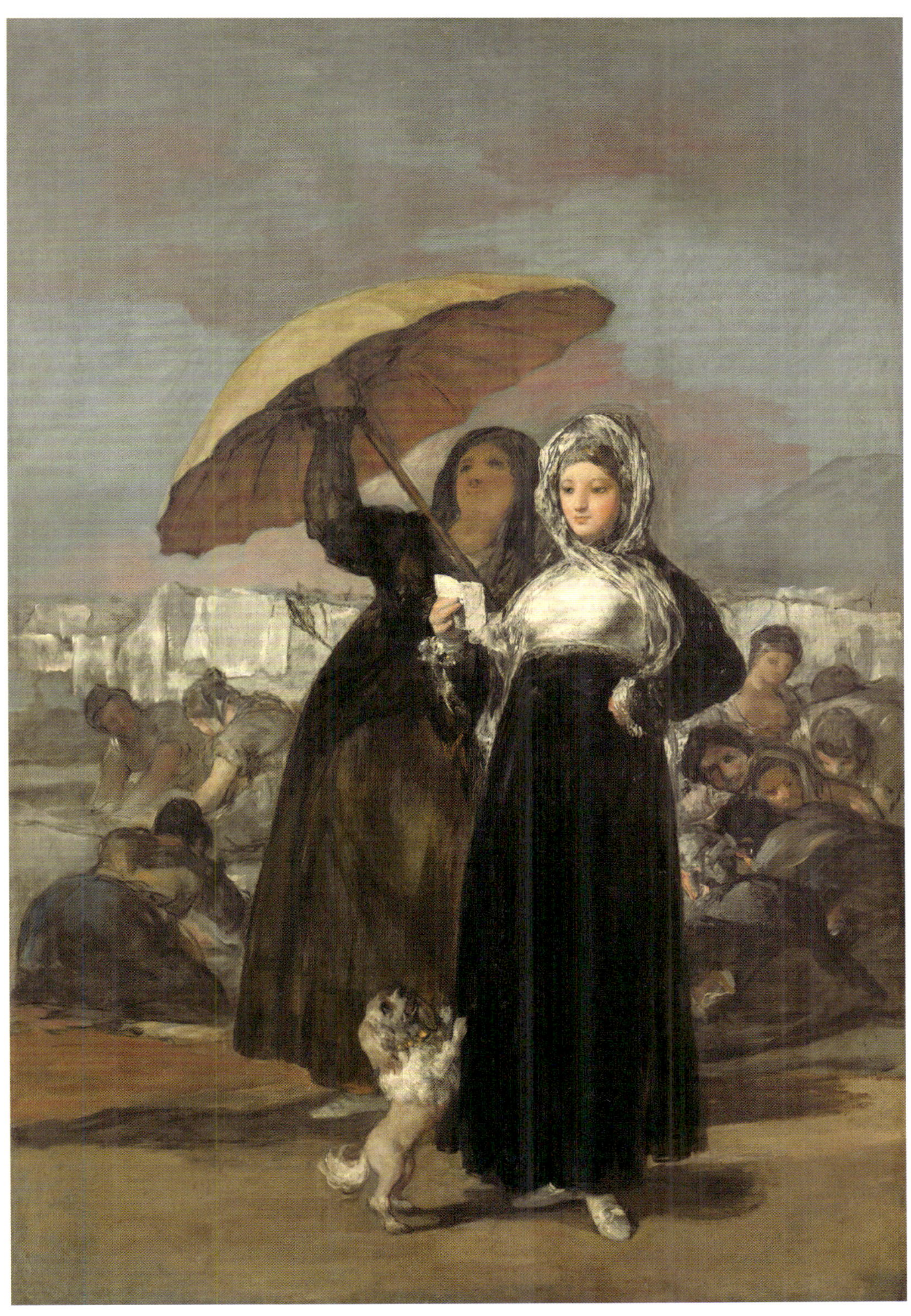

Fig. 24
Francisco de Goya y Lucientes
Time (*Le Temps*) or *The Old
Women* (*Les Vieilles*), ca. 1808–12
Oil on canvas
71¼ × 49 ¼ in. (181 × 125 cm)
Palais des Beaux-Arts, Lille

lower left corner of the painting, which reads "C. 104."[38] Bernice Davidson proposed that the number—not one of the *X* numbers found on paintings in the 1812 inventory—was added in 1836 when the painting was acquired by the French government.[39] The number, however, does not correspond to any known inventory or list of the paintings of Louis-Philippe's Galerie Espagnole and must, therefore, be linked to another collection. Further evidence makes this number even more mysterious. A matching number—"C. 103" in white paint—was discovered in the late 1980s in the lower left corner of Goya's *Young Women* (*Les Jeunes*), also known as *The Letter* (*La Lettre*) (fig. 23).[40] The subject of the painting is two women, full-length against a bright blue sky. The one in the foreground is dressed in the Spanish costume of a *maja*. A dog on its hind legs and pawing her skirt looks upward toward a letter she seems to be reading. Behind her, the other woman, dressed in black, holds up a large umbrella to protect her from the sun. The middle background and the horizon line are occupied by a number of people, at least ten, all of whom seem to be women. Kneeling on the ground and huddled together, they appear to be cleaning clothes in a body of water. Behind them, almost cutting the painting horizontally in two halves, are white garments and pieces of laundry, drying in the sun. The women seem to be from two very distinct social spheres: the ones in the foreground from the upper class and those in the background from the working class. What is the relationship between the two standing figures? Are they equals, or is the woman with the umbrella a lady-in-waiting? What is the content of the letter and why is it so prominent? And why are the two women juxtaposed with a depiction of laundry washing?

Like *The Forge*, the *Young Women* was sold by Javier Goya to Taylor and displayed in the Galerie Espagnole, and it was titled *Women of Madrid Dressed as Majas* (*Femmes de Madrid en costume de majas*).[41] *The Forge* was later bought by the dealer Farrer, while the *Young Women* was sold—together with other works by Goya, including a work known as *Time* (*Le Temps*) or the *Old Women* (*Les Vieilles*) (fig. 24)—to another dealer, Durlacher, for Henry Bulwer, 1st Baron Dalling and Bulwer (1801–1872). This canvas portrays two women, decrepit though bejeweled and fashionably dressed. The one on the right holds a miniature in her hand (possibly a portrait of herself as a young woman or of a loved one), while the other presents a mirror to her companion, with the inscription "Que tal?" (How are you?) on the back. The figure of a winged, bearded man behind them is an allegory of Time, which

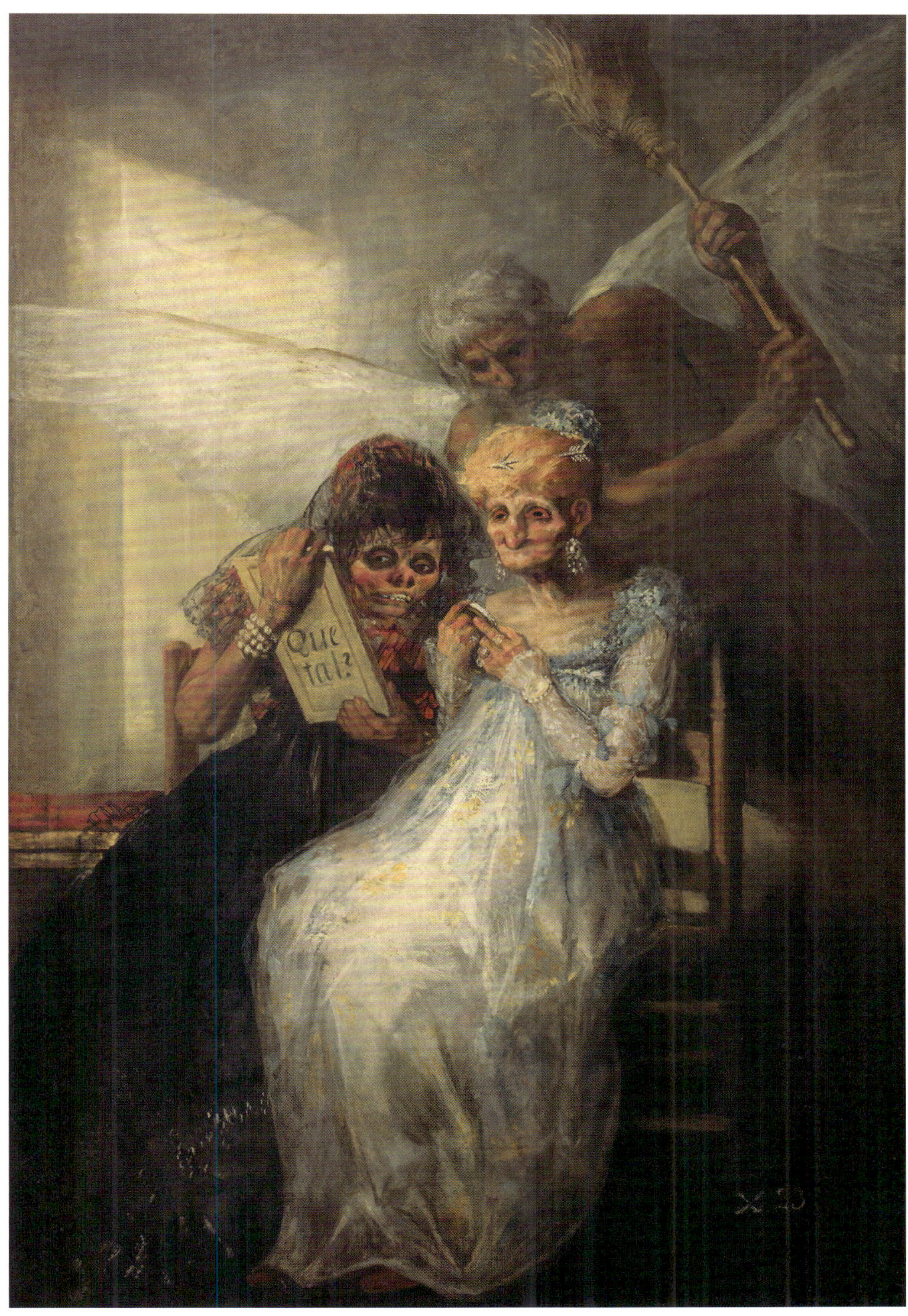

Que
tal?

has ravaged them. Most likely a *vanitas*, the painting focuses on the passing of time and the fleeting nature of youth and beauty. As with many works by Goya, this painting is tragic but also has a comic aspect. As revealed by the 1873 sale catalogue of Dalling and Bulwer's collection, it was he who paired and renamed the two paintings *Youth* and *Age*, calling the second a "companion" to the first one. Even if the dimensions are not given in the sale, it was certainly he who had the *Old Women* enlarged to make it into a pendant of the *Young Women*. The two pictures entered the museum in Lille, as pendants, in 1874, and have been considered as such until recently. They were not, however, intended by Goya to be seen together. While the *Young Women* first appears in 1836 (and has a *C* number), the *Old Women* is listed in the 1812 inventory and has an *X* number in the bottom right corner. Furthermore, as already mentioned, the dimensions of the *Old Women* were enlarged after 1853 to make it into a pendant of the *Young Women*.[42] While the *Old Women* is painted on a reused canvas (as we would expect from a painting created by Goya during the war), the *Young Women* is painted on a new canvas.

A number of factors suggest that the *Young Women* could, instead, be the pendant of *The Forge*. The two paintings are the same size, and technical analysis has proven that their original dimensions are the same.[43] They are painted on the same type of canvas, and both are made out of two pieces of canvas, joined selvage to selvage. The only difference is that while the *Young Women* is made out of an upper piece of canvas that is 85 cm high and a lower one that is 96 cm high, *The Forge* is made out of an upper piece of canvas that is 95.5 cm high and a lower one that is 86 cm high.[44] The construction of both canvases is identical, but they were used in different orientations. The types of grounds used in the two paintings are also identical. The oil preparation in both is gray, with a thicker lower layer, with coarsely ground particles, and a thinner upper layer with more finely ground particles. These similarities might suggest that they were intended as pendants.[45] While one canvas focuses on men, the other focuses on women, but both show people at work (smiths in the former and laundresses in the latter). However, aside from the dimensions and technique, there is nothing to suggest that a painting of elegant women reading a letter and holding a parasol and one of blacksmiths working in a forge are pendants. Moreover, the figures in the foreground of the two paintings are different in scale. The likely scenario is that a collector acquired both *The Forge* and the *Young Women*, possibly displaying them together, and gave them consecutive inventory numbers. Later on, the two paintings reached the Galerie Espagnole, together with *Old Women*; subsequently, the *Young Women* ended up being paired with the *Old Women* instead.

We know that the *X* numbers are linked to the 1812 inventory (*X* stands for Xavier, another spelling that Goya's son, Javier, used for his first name), but we do not know what the *C* numbers are linked to. They are not related to the Galerie Espagnole, and, since the two canvases were never again in the same collection after the dissolution of the Galerie Espagnole, the *C* numbers must predate 1836. This means that, at some point between the 1810s and 1836, *The Forge* and the *Young Women* belonged to the same person.

Until recently, it was believed that *The Forge* and the *Young Women* were the only two paintings with *C* numbers in white paint.[46] However, another work by Goya (and possibly two) had *C* numbers. A recent restoration has revealed that the half-length *St. Paul* (fig. 26), signed by Goya and dated to the early 1820s, has "C. 110" in the lower right corner.[47] The lettering of this inscription is consistent with the inventory numbers of *The Forge* and the *Young Women*, and the "0" in these inscriptions looks, characteristically, like a small "o." In Spain until the 1930s, the painting had belonged, by 1913, to the art dealer and collector Rafael García Palencia in Madrid. It was sold by Palencia's widow at the time of the Spanish Civil War, and by 1937 it was in London with Colnaghi & Co. The *St. Paul* has as a pendant the *St. Peter* (fig. 25), which was acquired by Duncan Phillips (1886–1966) in 1936.[48] There appears to be no inventory number on the *St. Peter*; however, the number may have been removed during a conservation treatment. It would be expected for the *St. Peter* to have a *C* number consecutive to the *St. Paul*—either C. 109 or C. 111. It therefore seems that before 1836 a single collector owned at least four paintings by Goya: *The Forge*, the *Young Women*, the *St. Peter*, and the *St. Paul*. This individual may have owned more paintings by Goya and potentially by other artists (no *C* numbers have been identified, so far, on works by other painters). The *C* may have stood for the initial of the collector, although no likely candidate can be identified at present. It could also refer to a location, or may have been an altogether arbitrary identifier linked to a specific document that used that letter as a marker. Until further evidence emerges around this puzzling collection, nothing can be determined about the history of *The Forge* before it entered the Galerie Espagnole of King Louis-Philippe.

Following pages:

Fig. 25
Francisco de Goya y Lucientes
St. Peter, ca. 1820–24
Oil on canvas
28¾ × 25¼ in. (73 × 64.1 cm)
The Phillips Collection,
Washington, DC

Fig. 26
Francisco de Goya y Lucientes
St. Paul, ca. 1820–24
Oil on canvas
28¾ × 25⅜ in. (73 × 64.5 cm)
Private collection

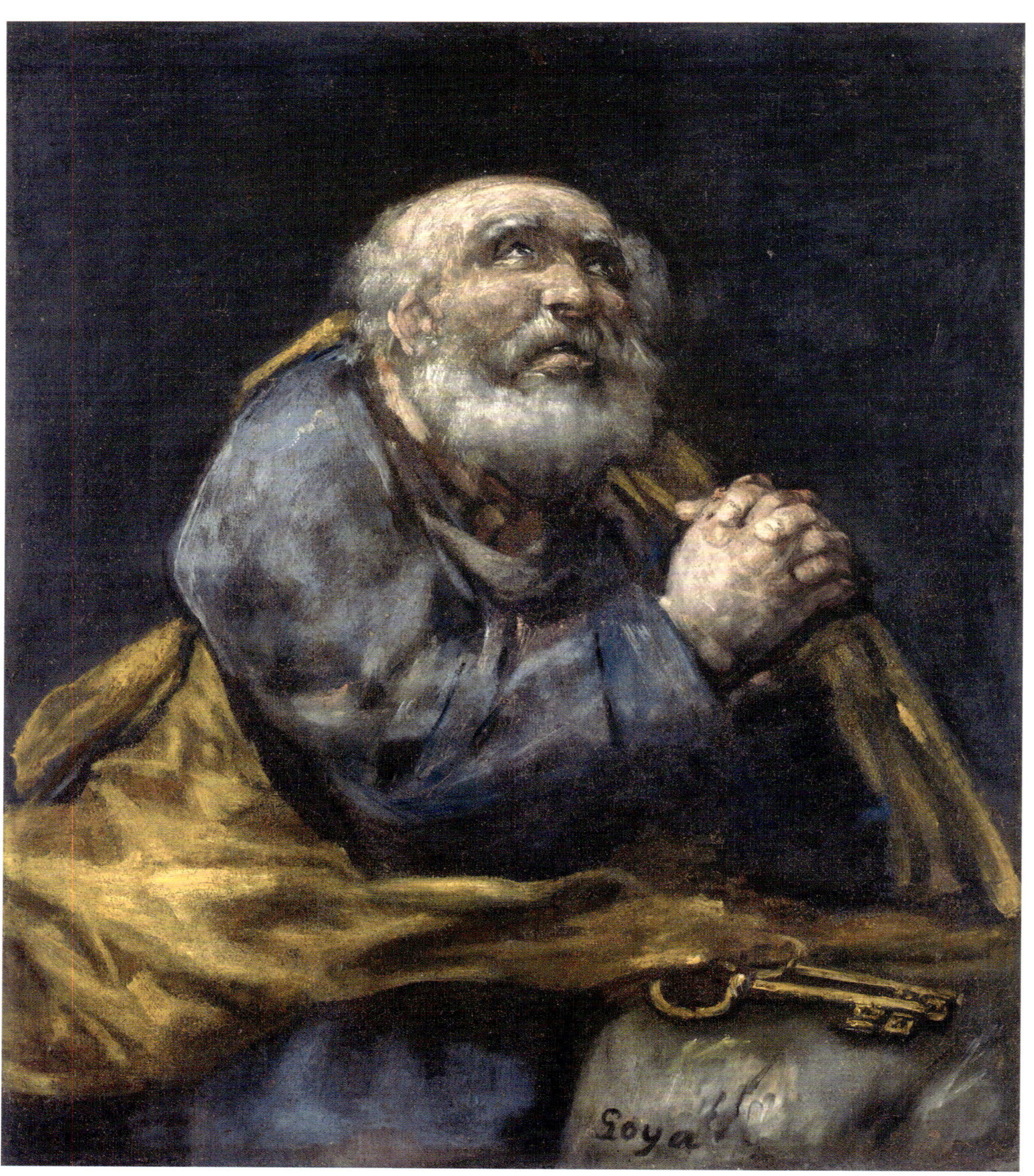
Goya

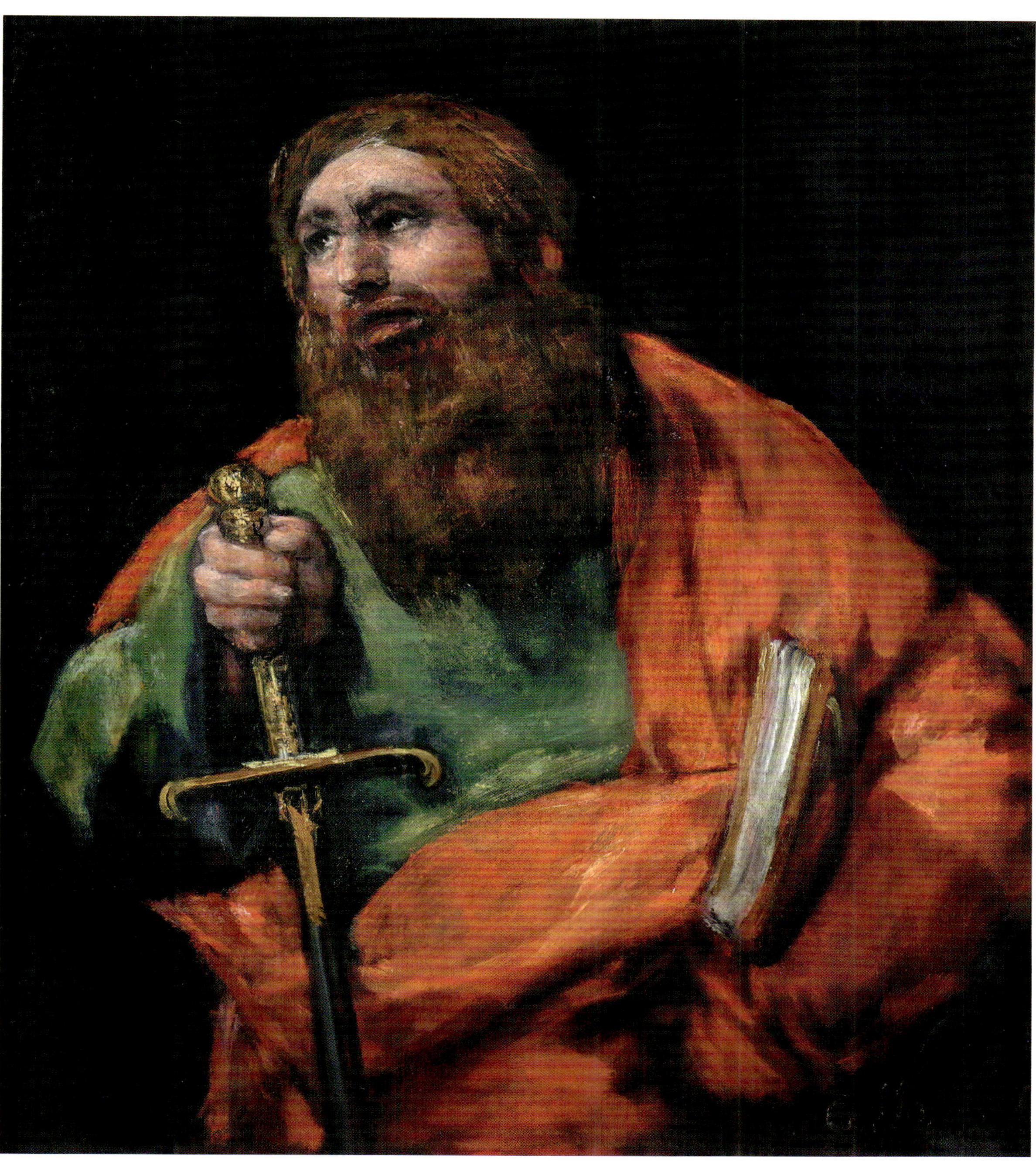

In 1848, ten years after the Galerie Espagnole at the Louvre opened, the revolution in France brought the downfall of Louis-Philippe, his abdication and exile in England. The Galerie Espagnole closed its doors on January 1, 1849, never to reopen. After the creation of the Second Republic, the ascent to power of Louis-Napoleon (later Emperor Napoleon III, 1808–1873), and Louis-Philippe's death, in 1850, the French government determined that the Spanish paintings at the Louvre, as private property of the deceased king, were to be returned to the Orléans family. In July 1851, the paintings were sent to England. Between May 6 and 21, 1853, the contents of the Galerie Espagnole were dispersed at an auction at Christie and Manson on King's Street in London. Goya's *Forge* was sold—as lot 354—to the dealer Henry T. Farrer (1798–1866) for £10.[49]

The Forge and Henry Clay Frick

Henry T. Farrer was most likely acting as an agent for the collector Henry Labouchere (after 1859, 1st Baron Taunton, 1798–1869) when he acquired *The Forge*.[50] The painting was inherited by Lord Taunton's daughter, Mary Dorothy Labouchere (d. 1920), wife of the politician Edward James Stanley (1826–1907), together with the Gothic Revival house Quantock Lodge (fig. 27), which his grandfather had built near Bridgewater, in Somerset. Mary and Edward had two sons—Henry Thomas (1873–1900) and Edward Arthur Vesey Stanley (1879–1941). After Henry's death in Africa, in the Second Boer War, the house and collection were inherited by Edward Arthur, Lord Taunton's grandson.

Financial difficulties compelled Edward Arthur Vesey Stanley to sell Quantock Lodge and its contents in 1919. However, some of the paintings from Lord Taunton's collection were sold before that. This was recalled by the British art historian and critic Robert Langton Douglas (1864–1951) in a letter of November 30, 1943, to Margaret E. Gilman at the Fogg Museum in Boston:

> In the year 1909, the late Captain E.A.V. Stanley asked me to make a catalogue of the collection of pictures at Quantock Lodge in Somerset, a collection that had been formed by his grandfather, Henry Labouchere, Lord Taunton. I had already found at Quantock Lodge many important pictures. Amongst these, were works by Perugino, Domenico Ghirlandajo, Rogier van

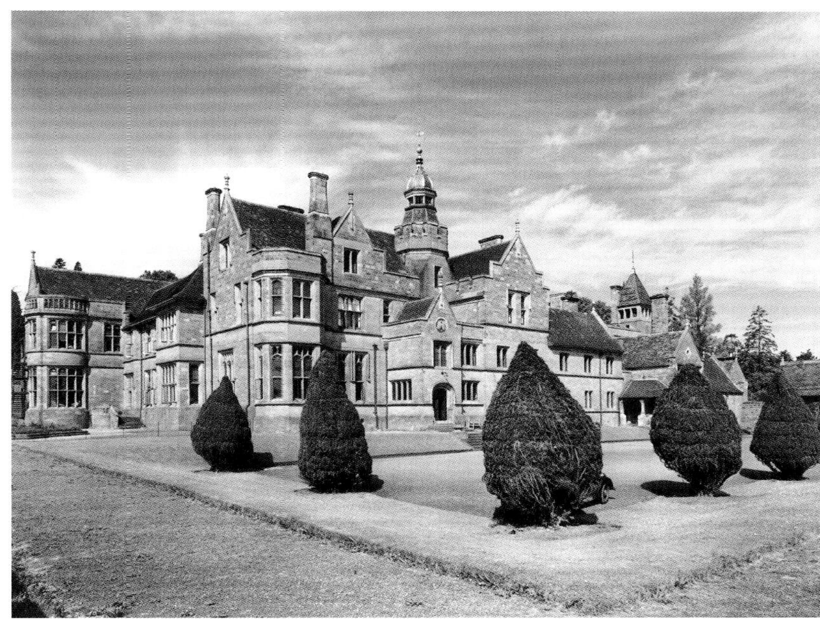

Fig. 27
Quantock Lodge, Somerset

der Weyden, El Greco, Rembrandt, Zurbaran and Goya, as well as a bust of Lorenzo de' Medici which is now at Washington.

Subsequently, Captain Stanley told me that he wished to sell some of the pictures in his collection. It was my desire from the first that the more important pictures should go to public galleries. The Director of the National Gallery had already seen the collection; but he had not bought any of the pictures. I then took Dr. Max Friedländer, who was at that time Dr. Bode's chief assistant, to Quantock Lodge. Subsequently, Mr. Edward Robinson of the Metropolitan Museum visited the collection with me; and he instructed me to buy a predella of a picture by Ghirlandajo for the Museum.

As I had not succeeded in disposing of any of the more important pictures to public galleries, I decided to communicate with Messrs. P. & D. Colnaghi; and I took the two partners of this firm to see them. In this way, two important pictures that were in the Quantock Lodge collection, *The Forge* by Goya, and the *Portrait of Vincentio Anastagi* by El Greco, ultimately found their way into the Frick Collection. Zurbaran's *Moorish Battle*, I bought myself, and sold it later on, to the Metropolitan Museum.[51]

In July 1914, *The Forge* was acquired by Colnaghi and Knoedler, and, by the end of the year, it had been purchased by Henry Clay Frick (1849–1919) in New York. On December 5, 1914, Frick was invoiced by Knoedler for six paintings: Joseph Mallord William Turner's *Harbor of Dieppe: Changement de Domicile*, Jacob Henricus Maris's *The Bridge*, Édouard Manet's *The Bullfight*, Edgar Degas's *The Rehearsal*, and two Goya canvases—the *Portrait of a Lady (María Martínez de Puga?)* and *The Forge*. The total amount for the six works was $457,500, but the two most expensive paintings in the group were Turner's *Harbor of Dieppe* ($175,000) and Goya's *Forge* ($125,000).[52] Of these six paintings, only *The Forge* came from Quantock Lodge: the invoice specified that the Goya had a provenance "from the Quantock Lodge Collection. Previously in the Collection of Lord Taunton and King Louis Philippe. Galerie Espagnole, No. 101."

In writing at least, Frick's comments regarding his acquisitions were laconic at best. According to his daughter, Helen Clay Frick (1888–1984), he only purchased paintings "that were pleasant to live with."[53] It is difficult to describe Goya's *Forge* as "pleasant." Within the Frick mansion's setting of walls covered with aristocratic effigies and peaceful landscapes, the large canvas by Goya showing three men performing backbreaking work stands out as atypical. The painting likely resonated with Frick in a number of—possibly contradictory—ways.

Frick was born to Swiss and German immigrants in western Pennsylvania.[54] As a young man, he worked in his maternal grandfather's whiskey distillery before focusing on the coke business. Understanding the importance of coke—bituminous coal that was baked in conical-shaped ovens—for the emerging steel industry, Frick began acquiring and building coke ovens and, by 1873, Frick and Company (renamed H. C. Frick and Company, in 1878) had two hundred coke ovens. By 1882, the company owned more than one thousand ovens and three thousand acres of coal land. By the age of thirty, in 1879, Frick (fig. 28) was a millionaire; by the early 1880s, his company was producing almost one million tons of coke per year.[55] In the 1880s, Frick became closely associated with Andrew Carnegie (1835–1919). Born into a poor family of Scottish immigrants who arrived in Pittsburgh in 1848, Carnegie would become one of the richest men in the world. His fortune derived from the production of steel—an alloy of iron, with a carbon content between 0.15 and 0.25 percent—which was stronger and more flexible than iron. Manufactured since the fifteenth century in Central Asia, and since the eighteenth century in Europe, steel, at the end of the nineteenth century in America, "took the form of rails, ships, I-beams for skyscrapers, endless miles

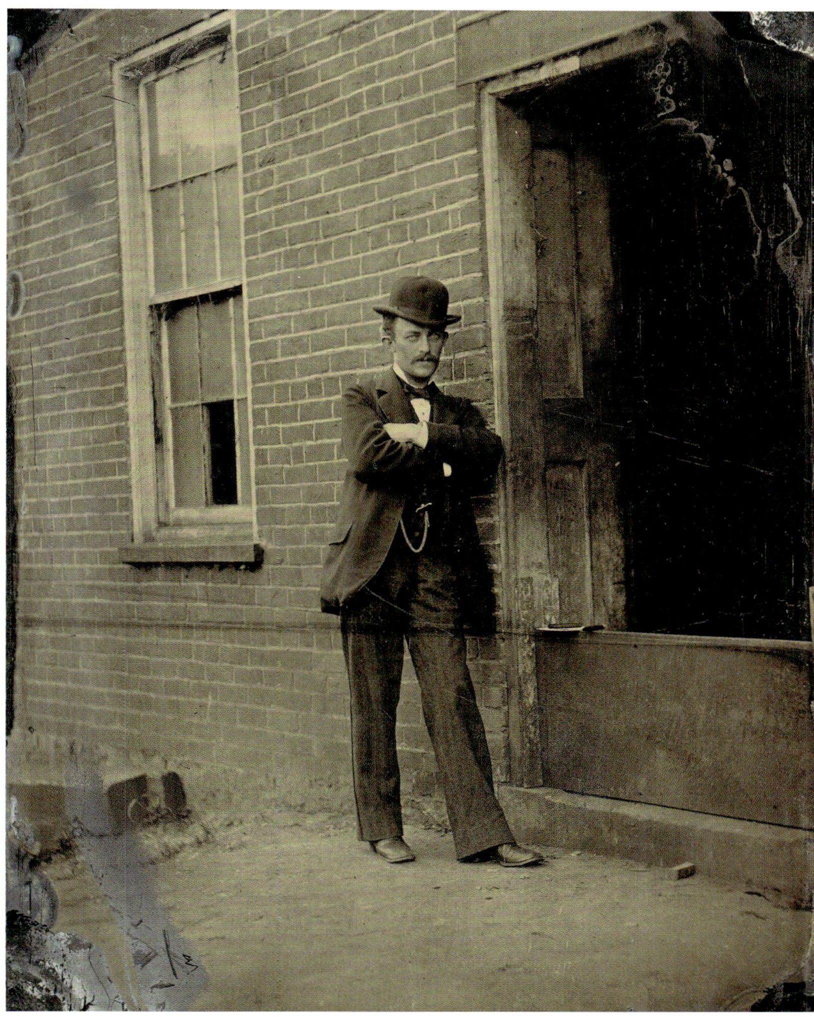

Fig. 28
Henry Clay Frick, ca. 1874.
The Frick Collection/Frick Art
Reference Library Archives

of cable and piping, machinery, armaments, and tin plate for cans, providing the medium with which and upon which the modern world was reshaping itself."[56] Thanks to the technological advances of the Industrial Revolution, which had started earlier in the century in the United Kingdom, large steel mills could be built in the United States; and in the late nineteenth century, the area of Pittsburgh became one of the prime producers of steel in the world. About 250,000 people at the time lived at the confluence between the Allegheny and Monongahela rivers, and most of them were involved in one way or another in the production of steel. By the late 1890s, "Pittsburgh would account for more than half of all the iron and steel made in the United States."[57] To create steel, Carnegie needed Frick's coke, and the two promptly partnered, becoming the most prominent American steel barons and millionaires. Together, they produced more than one million tons of steel annually.[58] On January 14, 1889, Henry Clay Frick became the chairman of Carnegie Brothers and Company.

By 1914, when Frick purchased Goya's *Forge*, his entire fortune derived from the production of coke and steel, the manufacture of which relied on technology and cheap labor. The men in the steel mills worked under much bleaker conditions than Goya's pre-industrial blacksmiths. In early June 1892, the *Pittsburgh Times* described one of these mills:

> When the steel is ready, the open hearth furnaces are tapped, and streams of molten steel run into the mold and the ingot is made. The weight varies from 20 to 100 tons. It is then . . . taken from the metal mold while still hot and is transferred on a special car to the press shop. This car has a capacity of 150 tons, five times that of the average freight car. At the press shop, two large cranes that could lift an ordinary house take this mountain of metal and put it in a furnace where it is heated . . . and is carried to the Armor rolling mill . . . a mill so vast that mere figures are powerless to convey a full appreciation of its size [fig. 29].[59]

The elaborate mills and equipment could be dangerous, and often fatal, to the men working there. The *Homestead Local News* reported one of many such incidents, in April 1892:

> When the blast is put on, it forces a terrific blaze containing particles of the molten steel, out against an iron shield. In the course of a few hours there is an accumulation of metal [referred to as "the skull"] on the shield or wall which of course is quite heavy and must be removed at frequent intervals, otherwise it would fall, which it did in this instance. . . . Passing somewhat underneath the shield is a pressure pipe. . . . When the skull fell, it struck the pipe referred to, causing the pressure to escape. Released from control, the vessel containing molten metal tipped over and emptied into the pit below where it came in contact with moisture, resulting in a terrific explosion. The metal was scattered in all directions, some of it striking the opposite wall seventy feet away. It is not surprising that many workmen were burned. Indeed the great wonder is that more were not fatally burned. The list is long enough however.[60]

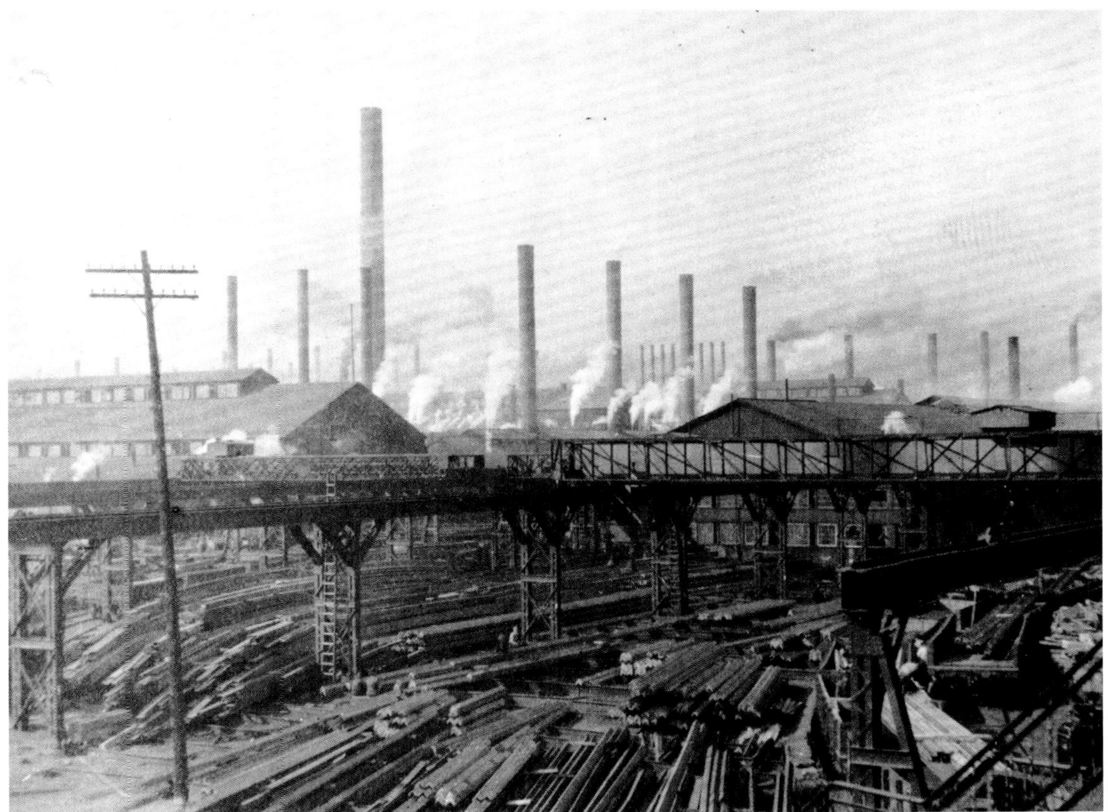
Fig. 29
Steel works in Pittsburgh, 1899.
The Frick Collection/Frick Art
Reference Library Archives

With owners of steel mills (and other industrial enterprises at the time) making fortunes on the backs of workers who put their lives at risk for pitiful wages, the workers started joining unions to negotiate for better salaries and working conditions.

Frick was one of the staunchest enemies of unions' efforts in the United States at the time, and hostilities came to a tragic head in the summer of 1892 at the Homestead Mill—built in 1881 on the banks of the Monongahela River, east of Pittsburgh—which belonged to Carnegie and was under Frick's management.[61] During that fateful summer, Carnegie was vacationing in his native Scotland. On August 4, 1876, three unions—the classically named United Sons of Vulcan; the Associated Brotherhood of Iron and Steel Heaters, Rollers, and Roughers of the United States; and the Iron and Steel Roll Hands Union, later joined by four other unions—merged as the Amalgamated Association of Iron and Steel Workers of the United States, becoming the "most powerful labor organization in the steel industry," with at least twenty-one thousand members.[62] The union represented only the skilled workers at the Homestead Mill; at around this time, it included roughly 800 of the 3,800 people working at Homestead. With the dissatisfaction about wages and labor conditions and the lack of dialogue with management, the union went on strike on June 29, 1892. Frick, adamantly refusing to engage with the union or even recognize its existence, had already started to defend the mill. He had done so by building physical defenses all around the plant (known popularly in Pittsburgh as "Fort Frick"), by engaging strikebreakers, and—most controversially of all—by hiring a private patrol, from the Pinkerton National Detective Agency, to defend the mill and the strikebreakers from the strikers.

Frick's actions that summer resulted in the "deadliest clash between workers and owners in American labor history" (fig. 30).[63] In the early hours of the morning of July 6, 1892, two barges—the *Iron Mountain* and the *Monongahela*—crossed the Monongahela River to Homestead with about three hundred Pinkerton agents, fully armed with pistols, Winchester rifles, and ammunition. The strikers were expecting the arrival of the Pinkertons, and in early July the *Pittsburgh Post* printed the headline "IT LOOKS LIKE WAR."[64] The clash between the workers and Pinkerton agents attempting to land resulted in armed combat that lasted well into the morning. The number of casualties varies according to the source, but at least three Pinkertons and seven workers (Peter Farris, John E. Morris, George W. Rutter, Joseph Sotak, Henry Striegel, Silas Wain, and Thomas Weldon) were killed.[65] Hundreds were wounded on both sides; it is not known how many of them died afterward. Later that day, the strikers marched the Pinkertons off the barges and through Homestead, running a "bloody gauntlet" that was described at the time by an eyewitness:

> [They entered] a lane formed by two long lines of infuriated men who did not act like human beings . . . they were beaten over the head with clubs and the butt ends of rifles. You could almost hear their skulls crack. They were kicked, knocked down and jumped upon. Their clothes were torn from their backs, and when they finally escaped it was with faces of ashen paleness and with the blood in streams rushing down the backs of their heads staining their clothes. It ran in rivulets down their faces, which in the melee they had covered with their hands.[66]

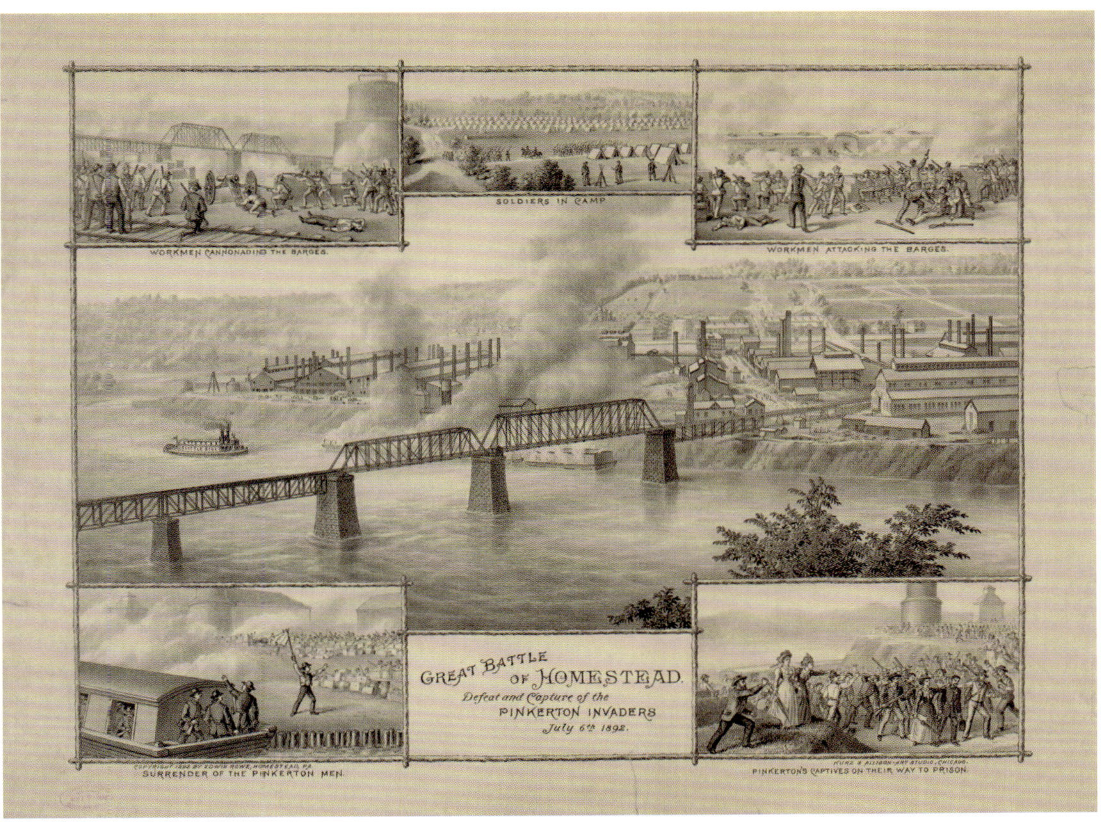

Fig. 30
Kurz and Allison Art Studio
Homestead Strike, 1892
Lithograph
Library of Congress Prints
and Photographs Division,
Washington, DC

The agents were brought to the Homestead opera house, detained there, and later, during the night, put on a train back to Pittsburgh. While it would be easy to see this as a battle between the working class and their capitalist oppressors, it should be noted that the Pinkertons were also poorly paid. One of them later said about the Homestead Battle: "We are working men ourselves and sympathize with the strikers now that we know the truth."[67]

Following the bloody events of July 6 and their aftermath, the governor of Pennsylvania called the National Guard, composed of thousands of members of the Pennsylvania State Militia, to re-establish order in Homestead. The strike, however, continued for a month, with Carnegie remaining absent, on holiday, and Frick refusing to acknowledge the existence of the union. Two further events of 1892 affected Frick profoundly. On July 23, around 2 p.m., while Frick sat in his office together with the company's vice-president, John G. A. Leishman (1857–1924), Alexander Berkman (1870–1936), a twenty-

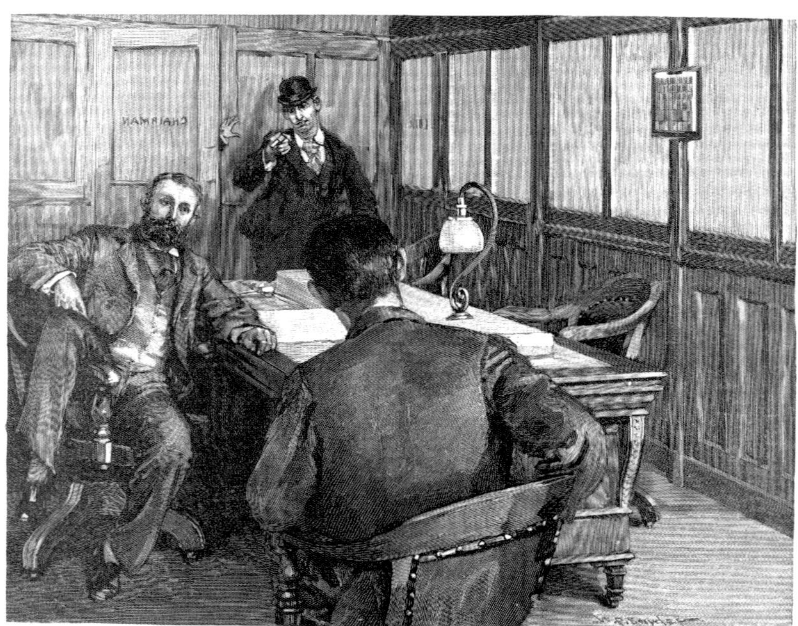

THE ATTEMPTED ASSASSINATION OF MR. FRICK.—Drawn by W. P. Snyder.

Fig. 31
"Assault Upon Mr. Frick,"
Harper's Weekly, August 6, 1892

five-year-old anarchist originally from Lithuania but based in Worcester, Massachusetts, busted into his office and attempted to kill him (fig. 31). Accounts differ, but Frick was shot at least once, maybe twice, and Berkman may have stabbed him, possibly three times, with a dagger made out of a steel file. The anarchist was also said to have had a capsule of fulminate of mercury in his mouth, ready to explode.[68] Berkman apparently acted on his own; the attempted assassination was in no way connected to the union and the strikers. Frick was not badly wounded, cabling Carnegie that same evening, "was shot twice but not dangerously." Berkman was arrested, put on trial, and sentenced to twenty-two years in prison (he was released in 1907).[69] A few days after the Homestead Battle, on July 8, Frick's wife Adelaide gave birth to the couple's fourth and last child, Henry Clay Frick Junior; but sadly the boy died less than a month after his birth, on August 3. So while Frick—whose second daughter, Martha, had died a year earlier—was recuperating at home from the attack on his life, he was also grieving the loss of Henry.

The Homestead Strike came to an end officially on November 21, 1892. The *Pittsburgh Post*'s headline was "THEY SURRENDER," and Frick wrote triumphantly to Carnegie, "Our victory is now complete and most gratifying. Do not think we will ever have any serious labor trouble again."[70] Notwithstanding the apparent victory, the Homestead Strike and Battle—combined with the assassination attempt and the loss of a second child—was the beginning of a long-lasting and deep rift between Frick and Carnegie that developed over the following years along with a number of other business issues. A definitive split between the two magnates occurred between 1898 and 1899; after legal action, the two settled in 1900, never to speak again. While Frick later moved to New York, in 1905, and focused more on collecting art, building his home to be eventually transformed into a public museum, he remained involved with the steel industry, through the United States Steel Corporation, until his death. When it came to the 1892 events at Homestead, Carnegie, later in life, claimed to regret what had happened: "Nothing I have ever had to meet in all my life . . . wounded me so deeply. No pangs remain of any wound . . . save that of Homestead."[71] As far as we know, Frick never mentioned the events of 1892 again in public or in private. It is, however, hard to believe that the bloodshed of the Homestead Battle, followed by a related (even if indirectly) assassination attempt, could have left any man altogether unmoved.

*   *   *

Discussing Goya's *Forge* in 1973, Fred Licht wrote that "one must keep the vagaries of art collectors in mind. After all, who would have thought that a painting such as this would eventually come to rest in the collection of a man whose interests in metallurgy were totally inimical to the ideals expressed in the painting?"[72] Beside what the "ideals" represented in Goya's *Forge* may or may not be, it is difficult to believe that the display of a painting of this subject matter did not have an effect on Henry Clay Frick. The three men working around an anvil are the ancestors of the steel workers in the Pittsburgh mills. Frick would have had, in front of him, every day, the image of those workers, on whom his fortune was based. To this day, the painting at the Frick serves as a monument to the genius of Goya but, at the same time, as a commemoration of the smiths and metalworkers who allowed Frick to build his wealth and, through it, an extraordinary art collection for public consumption. We will never know what went through Frick's mind when looking at *The Forge*, but for the public today the sacrifices of generations of metalworkers in the American steel industry are indelibly connected to the presence of this masterpiece in The Frick Collection.[73]

Notes

1 Kristof 1993, 176, 192.

2 *Catalogue* 1916, 71.

3 Shoolman and Slatkin 1942, 474.

4 Eitner 1986, 69.

5 Licht 1973, 23.

6 Alford 1960, 491.

7 Hughes 2003, 275.

8 Gassier and Wilson-Bareau 1981, 245; Brinton 1915, 88.

9 Goya's most recent and most complete biography is Tomlinson 2020. The information from this biographical sketch is entirely sourced from Tomlinson's book.

10 Tomlinson 2020, 289.

11 For the inventory, see J. Wilson-Bareau in Gassier and Wilson-Bareau 1971, 381; Wilson-Bareau 1996; V. Gerard Powell in Agen 2020, 202–9.

12 For Goya during the Peninsular War, see Madrid 2008.

13 The suggestion by Baticle and Marinas (1981, 86) that *The Forge* may appear in the 1812 inventory as a companion to a *Water-Seller* (these entries are usually linked to the Budapest *Water-Seller* and *Knife-Grinder*) is unconvincing.

14 Gassier and Wilson-Bareau 1971, 266; Gudiol 1971, 339, no. 682; De Angelis 1974, 128, no. 572; De Angelis and Gassier 1990, 128–29, no. 572.

15 Sánchez Cantón 1964, 97.

16 Brinton 1915, 89; Beruete 1917, 132; Wehle 1941, 22; *Handbook* 1947, 26, 29; *Catalogue* 1949, 279; Gudiol 1966, 148; Davidson 1968, 296; Davidson, Munhall, and Tscherny 1990, 115; Morales y Martín 1994, 341, no. 481; Munhall 1999, 102; Galassi 2012, 126; J. Portús in Madrid 2023, 53. A. Norton (in New York 1992, 154–57) provided the broadest date range for the painting, between 1812 and 1819.

17 Tomlinson 2020, 102.

18 Lafuente Ferrari (1947, 89) linked the Tintoretto painting to Goya's.

19 For such paintings, and depictions of forges in the nineteenth century, see Kristof 1993.

20 Kristof 1993, 177.

21 M. Armstrong Roche in Madrid, Boston, and New York 1988–89, 334.

22 Hughes 2003, 285.

23 For Album F, see Sayre 1958; Gassier and Wilson-Bareau 1971, 234–36, 238–39; Gassier 1973, 385–88; E. A. Sayre in Madrid, Boston, and New York 1988–89, cxx–cxxi; J. Wilson-Bareau in London 2001, 17–18, 91–92; Madrid 2019, 185–97; New York 2021, 168–69, 176–203; M. McDonald in Basel 2021, 309–14.

24 For the drawing and its links to *The Forge*, see Poore 1938, 160; Wehle 1941, 12; Hyatt Mayor 1946, 106; M. Armstrong Roche in Madrid, Boston, and New York 1988–89, 334, cat. 150.

25 Chicago 1941, 120.

26 This was already suggested by Hyatt Mayor 1974, 231: "I have assumed that the drawing came first, but it is possible that it did not."

27 Licht 1973, 22–23.

28 For the paintings, see D. Ekserdjian in London 2010, 268–69, nos. 177–78.

29 For this proposal, see D. Ekserdjian in London 2010, 268.

30 Gudiol 1941, 116.

31 *Catalogue* 1949, 278.

32 *Catalogue* 1949, 279.

33 "mission scientifique"; Lerner 2014, 101.

34 For Taylor's travels, see Luxenberg 2013.

35 For the Galerie Espagnole, see Baticle and Marinas 1981; Baticle 2003; Luxenberg 2008; Lerner 2014.

36 *Notice* 1838, 30, no. 101.

37 Baticle and Marinas 1981, 86; V. Gerard Powell in Agen 2020, 210–15. The other paintings by Goya that formed part of the group were the portrait of the Duchess of Alba (fig. 3), the *Majas on a Balcony*, *Lazarillo de Tormes* (fig. 14), *The Young Women* (*Les Jeunes*), or *The Letter* (*La Lettre*) (fig. 24), *The Old Women* (*Les Vieilles*), or *Time* (*Le Temps*) (fig. 25), and two lost paintings: the *Imperial Eagle Flying over Spain* and the *Last Prayer of the Condemned Man*.

38 Davidson 1968, 296.

39 Davidson 1968, 298n.1.

40 For the painting, see, most recently, A. Norton in New York 1992, 154–57, no. 35; D. Dujardin in Lille 2021–22, 54–63; M. A. Herradón in Milan 2023–24, 104–5.

41 Baticle 1992, 383–85. For the mention in the Galerie Espagnole, see V. Gerard Powell in Agen 2020, 212.

42 A. Norton in New York 1992, 152–54, no. 34; D. Dujardin in Lille 2021–22, 104–9.

43 Mottin and Chastel-Rousseau 2022, 90–97. The technical information about both paintings is provided in two unpublished reports, both available in the Frick's curatorial files. The examination report on *The Forge* by Dorothy Mahon, of the Metropolitan Museum of Art Paintings Conservation Department, dates from 2012–13. The report on the *Young Women* was written by Bruno Mottin, Eric Laval, and Myriam Eveno from the Centre de Recherche et de Restauration des Musées de

France and dates from February 10, 2022. I would like to particularly thank Dorothy Mahon and Bruno Mottin for all their help in discussing the examinations of both paintings.

44 Both paintings have been relined, and this accounts for the very slight variations in dimensions.

45 Most recently, see J. A. Tomlinson in Madrid and Washington 2002, 20, 244: "This would seem to be the pairing intended by the artist. Both these works—in contrast to the series of large genre scenes included in the 1812 inventory—are painted on new canvases, which might suggest they were painted after the conclusion of the Napoleonic War in Spain, when supplies such as canvas again became available."

46 For example, the unpublished report by the Centre de Recherche et de Restauration des Musées de France, dated February 10, 2022, commented that "on ne connaît aucun autre tableau du maître portant cette numération."

47 For the *St. Paul*, see Mayer 1937, 138; Gassier and Wilson-Bareau 1971, 329, no. 1642; De Angelis 1974, 134, no. 642.

48 For the *St. Peter*, see Gassier and Wilson-Bareau 1971, 329, no. 1641; De Angelis 1974, 134, no. 641; M. Moreno de las Heras in Madrid, Boston, and New York 1988–89, 275–76, no. 72.

49 Louis-Philippe sale 1853, 45, lot 354. V. Gerard Powell in Agen 2020, 212.

50 For the provenance of *The Forge*, see New York 1915, 16; Davidson 1968, 296.

51 The letter is preserved in the Frick's curatorial files.

52 The Maris was $54,000, the Goya portrait and the Degas were $45,000 each, and the Manet was $13,500.

53 Munhall 1999, 102.

54 For a biography of Frick, see Harvey 1936.

55 Standiford 2005, 55–56.

56 Standiford 2005, 25–26.

57 Standiford 2005, 26.

58 Standiford 2005, 27.

59 Standiford 2005, 133–34.

60 Standiford 2005, 113–14.

61 For the Homestead Strike, see Harvey 1936, 106–35; Krause 1992; Sanger 1998, 178–87; Standiford 2005.

62 Standiford 2005, 110–11.

63 Standiford 2005, 28.

64 Standiford 2005, 132.

65 The names of the deceased workers are commemorated in the Homestead Strike Victims Historical Marker between St. Mary's Cemetery and Homestead Cemetery, at the crossing of East 22nd Street and Main Street in Munhall, Pennsylvania. The names of the deceased Pinkertons are not recorded.

66 Standiford 2005, 176–77.

67 Standiford 2005, 179.

68 For accounts of the attempted murder, see Harvey 1936, 136–45; Sanger 1998, 189–95; Standiford 2005, 208–11.

69 Standiford 2005, 211.

70 Standiford 2005, 233.

71 Standiford 2005, 298.

72 Licht 1973, 23. Most recently, such links were also explored by Bianchi 2021.

73 For public responses to *The Forge* at the Frick, see Himes and Henningsen 2020, 134.

BIBLIOGRAPHY

Agen 2020 Juliet Wilson-Bareau and Bruno Mottin, eds. *Goya, génie d'avant-garde: Le maître et son école*. Exh. cat. Agen (Musée des Beaux-Arts), 2020.

Alford 1960 Alford, Roberta M. "Francisco Goya and the Intentions of the Artist." *Journal of Aesthetics and Art Criticism* 18 (1960): 482–93.

Basel 2021 Martin Schwander, ed. *Goya*. Exh. cat. Basel (Fondation Beyeler), 2021.

Baticle 1992 Baticle, Jeannine. *Goya*. Paris, 1992.

Baticle 2003 Baticle, Jeannine. "The Galerie Espagnole of Louis-Philippe." In *Manet/Velázquez: The French Taste for Spanish Paintings*, edited by Gary Tinterow and Geneviève Lacambre, 175–89. Exh. cat. Paris (Musée d'Orsay) and New York (The Metropolitan Museum of Art), 2003.

Baticle and Marinas 1981 Baticle, Jeannine, and Cristina Marinas. *La Galerie espagnole de Louis-Philippe au Louvre, 1838– 1848*. Paris, 1981.

Beruete 1917 Beruete, Aureliano de. *Goya: Composiciones y figuras*. Madrid, 1917.

Bianchi 2021 Bianchi, Tom. "Francisco de Goya y Lucientes, *The Forge*." In *The Sleeve Should Be Illegal & Other Reflections of Art at the Frick*, edited by Michaelyn Mitchell, 20–21. New York, 2021.

Brinton 1915 Brinton, Christian. "Goya and Certain Goyas in America." *Art in America* 3 (1915): 85–103.

Catalogue **1916** *Pictures in the Collection of Henry Clay Frick, at One East Seventieth Street, New York*. New York, 1916.

Catalogue **1949** *The Frick Collection: An Illustrated Catalogue of the Works of Art in the Collection of Henry Clay Frick*. Pittsburgh, 1949.

Chicago 1941 Daniel Catton Rich, ed. *The Art of Goya: Paintings, Drawings and Prints*. Exh. cat. Chicago (The Art Institute of Chicago), 1941.

Davidson 1968 Davidson, Bernice, et al. *The Frick Collection: An Illustrated Catalogue*. Vol. 2, *Paintings: French, Italian, and Spanish*. New York, 1968.

Davidson, Munhall, and Tscherny 1990 Davidson, Bernice, Edgar Munhall, and Nadia Tscherny. *Paintings from The Frick Collection*. New York, 1990.

De Angelis 1974 De Angelis, Rita. *L'opera pittorica completa di Goya*. Milan, 1974.

De Angelis and Gassier 1990 De Angelis, Rita, and Paul Gassier. *Tout l'oeuvre peint de Goya*. Paris, 1990.

Eitner 1986 Eitner, Lorenz. *An Outline of 19th Century European Painting: From David through Cézanne*. New York, 1986.

Galassi 2012 Galassi, Susan Grace. "Henry Clay Frick's Galerie Espagnole." In *Collecting Spanish Art: Spain's Golden Age and America's Gilded Age*, edited by Inge Reist and José Luis Colomer, 125–47. New York, 2012.

Gassier 1973 Gassier, Pierre. *The Drawings of Goya: The Complete Albums*. London, 1973.

Gassier and Wilson-Bareau 1971 Gassier, Pierre, and Juliet Wilson-Bareau. *The Life and Complete Work of Francisco Goya*. New York, 1971.

Gassier and Wilson-Bareau 1981 Gassier, Pierre, and Juliet Wilson-Bareau. *The Life and Complete Work of Francisco Goya*. New York, 1981.

Gudiol 1941   Gudiol, José. *Goya*. New York, 1941.

Gudiol 1966   Gudiol, José. *Goya*. London, 1966.

Gudiol 1971   Gudiol, José. *Goya 1746–1828: Biography, Analytical Study and Catalogue of His Paintings*. Barcelona, 1971.

Handbook 1947   *The Frick Collection: Handbook*. New York, 1947.

Harvey 1936   Harvey, George. *Henry Clay Frick: The Man*. New York, 1936.

Himes and Henningsen 2020   Himes, Rachel, and Caitlin F. Henningsen. "Looking at Art, Regarding History: Gallery Teaching in a Gilded Age Mansion." *Journal of Museum Education* 45 (2020): 127–38.

Hughes 2003   Hughes, Robert. *Goya*. New York, 2003.

Hyatt Mayor 1946   Hyatt Mayor, Alpheus. "Goya's Creativeness." *Metropolitan Museum of Art Bulletin* 5 (1946): 105–9.

Hyatt Mayor 1974   Hyatt Mayor, Alpheus. *Goya: 67 Drawings*. New York, 1974.

Krause 1992   Krause, Paul. *The Battle for Homestead, 1880–1892: Politics, Culture, and Steel*. Pittsburgh and London, 1992.

Kristof 1993   Kristof, Jane. "Blacksmiths, Weavers and Artists: Images of Labor in the Nineteenth Century." *Nineteenth-Century Contexts* 17 (1993): 174–203.

Lafuente Ferrari 1947   Lafuente Ferrari, Enrique. *Antecedentes, coincidencias e influencias del arte de Goya*. Madrid, 1947.

Lerner 2014   Lerner, Bettina. "Collecting for Clio: Louis-Philippe's Musée Espagnol or the Louvre as National History." *L'Esprit Créateur* 54 (2014): 101–14.

Licht 1973   Licht, Fred. *Goya in Perspective*. Englewood Cliffs, NJ, 1973.

Lille 2021–22   Donatienne Dujardin and Régis Cotentin, eds. *Expérience Goya*. Exh. cat. Lille (Palais des Beaux-Arts), 2021–22.

London 2001   Juliet Wilson-Bareau, ed. *Goya: Drawings from His Private Albums*. Exh. cat. London (Hayward Gallery), 2001.

London 2010   David Ekserdjian, ed. *Treasures from Budapest: European Masterpieces from Leonardo to Schiele*. London (Royal Academy of Arts), 2010.

Louis-Philippe sale 1853   *Catalogue des tableaux formant la célèbre Galerie Espagnole de S.M. feu le Roi Louis Philippe*. Sale cat. Christie and Manson, London, May 6–7, 13–14, 20–21, 27–28, 1853.

Luxenberg 2008   Luxenberg, Alisa. *The Galerie Espagnole and the Museo Nacional, 1835–1853*. Burlington, VT, 2008.

Luxenberg 2013   Luxenberg, Alisa. *Secrets and Glory: Baron Taylor and His Voyage pittoresque en Espagne*. Madrid, 2013.

Madrid 2008   Manuela B. Mena Marqués, ed. *Goya en tiempos de guerra*. Exh. cat. Madrid (Museo Nacional del Prado), 2008.

Madrid 2016   Elena M. Santiago Páez, ed. *Ceán Bermúdez: Historiador del arte y coleccionista ilustrado*. Exh. cat. Madrid (Biblioteca Nacional de España), 2016.

Madrid 2019   Manuela B. Mena Marqués, ed. *Goya: Dibujos: Solo la voluntad me sobra*. Exh. cat. Madrid (Museo Nacional del Prado), 2019.

Madrid 2023   Javier Portús, ed. *Obras maestras españolas de la Frick Collection*. Exh. cat. Madrid (Museo Nacional del Prado), 2023.

Madrid, Boston, and New York 1988–89   Alfonso E. Pérez-Sánchez and Eleanor A. Sayre, eds. *Goya and the Spirit of Enlightenment*. Exh. cat. Madrid (Museo Nacional del Prado), Boston (Museum of Fine Arts), and New York (The Metropolitan Museum of Art), 1988.

Madrid and Washington 2002   Janis A. Tomlinson, ed. *Goya: Images of Women*. Exh. cat. Madrid (Museo Nacional del Prado) and Washington (National Gallery of Art), 2002.

Mayer 1937   Mayer, August L. "A Late Goya." *Burlington Magazine* 71 (1937): 138–39.

Milan 2023–24   Victor Nieto Alcaide, ed. *Goya: La ribellione della ragione*. Exh. cat. Milan (Palazzo Reale), 2023–24.

Morales y Martín 1994   Morales y Martín, José Luis. *Goya: Catalogo de la pintura*. Zaragoza, 1994.

Mottin and Chastel-Rousseau 2022   Mottin, Bruno, and Charlotte Chastel-Rousseau. "Goya peintre." *Technè* 53 (2022): 3–123.

Munhall 1999   Munhall, Edgar, ed. *The Frick Collection: A Tour*. New York, 1999.

New York 1915   *Catalogue: Loan Exhibition of Paintings by El Greco and Goya for the Benefit of the American Women War Relief Fund and the Belgian Relief Fund*. Exh. cat. New York (M. Knoedler & Co.), 1915.

New York 1992   *Masterworks from the Musée des Beaux-Arts, Lille*. Exh. cat. New York (The Metropolitan Museum of Art), 1992.

New York 2021   Mark McDonald, ed. *Goya's Graphic Imagination*. Exh. cat. New York (The Metropolitan Museum of Art), 2021.

***Notice* 1838**   *Notice des tableaux de la Galerie Espagnole exposés dans les salles du Musée Royal au Louvre*. Paris, 1838.

Poore 1938   Poore, Charles. *Goya*. New York and London, 1938.

Sánchez Cantón 1964   Sánchez Cantón, Francisco Javier. *The Life and Works of Goya*. Madrid, 1964.

Sanger 1998   Sanger, Martha Frick Symington. *Henry Clay Frick: An Intimate Portrait*. New York, London, and Paris, 1998.

Sayre 1958   Sayre, Eleanor A. "An Old Man Writing. A Study of Goya's Albums." *Bulletin of the Museum of Fine Arts, Boston* 56 (1958): 116–29.

Shoolman and Slatkin 1942   Shoolman, Regina, and Charles E. Slatkin. *The Enjoyment of Art in America*. Philadelphia and New York, 1942.

Standiford 2005   Standiford, Les. *Meet You in Hell: Andrew Carnegie, Henry Clay Frick, and the Bitter Partnership That Transformed America*. New York, 2005.

Tomlinson 2020   Tomlinson, Janis A. *Goya: A Portrait of the Artist*. Princeton and Oxford, 2020.

Wehle 1941   Wehle, Harry B. *Fifty Drawings by Francisco Goya*. New York, 1941.

Wilson-Bareau 1996   Wilson-Bareau, Juliet. "Goya and the X Numbers: The 1812 Inventory and Early Acquisitions of 'Goya' Pictures." *Metropolitan Museum of Art Journal* 31 (1996): 159–74.

INDEX